A. C. Becker's

Redfish:

How, When & Where

A. C. Becker's
Redfish

How, When & Where

By A. C. Becker, Jr.

BOZKABOOKS

3334 Richmond, Suite 120
Houston, Texas 77098
713/522-FISH

A. C. Becker's Redfish: How, When & Where. Copyright© 1989 by A. C. Becker, Jr. All rights reserved. Bound and printed in Dallas, Texas. No part of this book may be reproduced, stored in a retrieval system or transmitted in any form, by any type of electronic, mechanical or copy technique without the prior written permission of the publisher, except by a reviewer, who may quote brief passages in a review.

Published by
BOZKABOOKS

First printing, July, 1989

Cover illustration by Mark Mantell

Layout and cover design by John Hillenbrand

ISBN:0-929980-02-6

This book is dedicated to the two people
who had to put up with the most headaches because
of my work habits when I become involved in writing projects.
First, my wife, June, who knew when not to call ''Honey do
this,'' and my publisher, Larry Bozka, who took the risks,
offered encouragement and edited the works to make it more
readable. Without them, *''Redfish: How, When & Where''*
would have been a chore, not a joy.

CONTENTS

FOREWORD

The first printing of *A.C. Becker's Speckled Trout: How, When & Where* rolled off the presses in November of 1988. Six weeks later, we put the show on the road.

The Texas boat show circuit begins in early January. Houston was first, followed by San Antonio and Dallas. In April we wrapped it up with the Houston Fishing Show, held each year at the George Brown Convention Center.

The days passed like a blur, each one a new experience. We spoke with literally thousands of fishermen from virtually all walks of life.

Most of all, we listened.

Big companies spend big bucks, sometimes hundreds of thousands of dollars, on sophisticated market surveys that give them a better understanding of their customers' needs. Some mail surveys; others use the telephone. Those that aren't particularly concerned about angering their audience go so far as to let a computer make the calls.

A.C. and I, however, have long contended that there's no substitute for personal contact ... a handshake, a smile, an open mind and an open ear.

The aforementioned boat show tour did nothing but reinforce that belief.

We saw a lot of old friends, and made many more new ones. And when we wrapped it up, we began to implement a priority list based upon what we had learned.

The popularity of saltwater fishing is without question on the rise. So is the demand for practical information on how to go about it. This book, and the flounder fishing title which comes next in the series, exist to fill that need.

A.C. Becker's Redfish: How, When & Where, is the eleventh book the author has penned in his 46-year career as a professional outdoor journalist. Like its predecessor, it's a reference book, complete with a detailed index.

To the greatest degree possible, we have strived to present the information in a format that is not only easy to read, but also easy to find. A.C.'s straightforward writing style is the nucleus of that format.

Speckled Trout is now in its second printing, and has won praise from fishermen and outdoor writers throughout the entire Gulf Coast. The first edition of 3,000 copies sold out in less than four months.

The need for coastal fishing information is indeed there, and I for one feel there's no one better suited to the job of teaching than A.C. Becker, Jr. Persons who have attended one of the author's instructional seminars would no doubt agree.

These seminars, again, were inspired by our experiences at boat shows. A.C.'s one-hour fishing clinic at the Houston Boat Show drew a standing-room-only crowd, and would have lasted all night had we not been asked to clear the room for the cleaning crew.

On May 6, we broke new ground with a one-day speckled trout fishing seminar held at the Nassau Bay Hilton and Marina in Clear Lake, Texas. For six hours, A.C. presented the facts, fielded questions, and shared his knowledge with an enthusiastic audience of speckled trout addicts.

The event was videotaped, and is the basis of a unique instructional video that is breaking some new ground of its own.

This book represents over five decades of experience and research. From one standpoint, it substantially reduces the need for trial-and-error. From the other, it sets the stage for a great deal more.

Fishing is by no means an exact science. For almost every rule there's an exception, and for every technique or theory there's an alternative. The angler who experiments is the one who will eventually succeed.

That, as much as anything, is what makes the sport of fishing such a pleasurable challenge.

Larry Bozka   Houston, Texas

INTRODUCTION

No question about it, the speckled trout, or "spotted seatrout" as biologists prefer to call it, is the queen of inshore Gulf of Mexico gamefish.

Beautifully marked, the fish is regal in appearance. It is a challenge to catch and it fights with authority. The speck is the backbone fish of most of the surf and tidal waters fishing tourna-

ments held in Gulf Coast states.

If the speckled trout is the queen, then the redfish, which marine biologists call the "red drum," has to be the king of these same inshore waters. The redfish is a handsome fish, though not as vividly marked as the speckled trout. It is more challenging to catch than the speckled trout, and because it grows so much larger than the speck, it is a much stronger and more determined fighter.

Every Gulf Coast state in which redfish can be caught has a maximum keeper length on the fish. It varies from state to state, and likely will be changed from time to time as the population of this popular gamefish fluctuates. At the time of this writing, the maximum keeper length in most Gulf Coast states is 28 inches. At least one Gulf state still has a 35-inch maximum keeper length, and along the Atlantic Coast, which falls within the historic range of this fish, it is still legal to retain one mature redfish a day.

Oversize redfish are legal to catch in those states with a maximum length limit, but the fish must be immediately returned to the water. Interpretation of the word "immediately" is what muddies the picture.

Some people consider "immediately" to mean right after the fish is hung up for pictures and then released. Fish kept out of the water for more than five minutes are very unlikely to survive, and it generally takes longer than that to hang up the fish, pose with it and have a buddy snap the photo. Chances are, too, that the buddy will also want his photo taken with the fish.

So what's the big deal about immediately returning the fish to the water? After all, the loss is but a single fish.

Not quite so.

Almost every redfish in excess of 30 inches is a female, in spite of the fact that most fishermen refer to them as "bull" reds. Every big bull that fails to survive is one less to spawn and propagate the species. At this time, in fact for the last two decades, the redfish population has been declining.

Back to that "bull" for a few comments. Exactly how "bull" came into the provincial name of the redfish is uncertain.

Normally, "bull" is used to describe the male of most species of wildlife. I suspect the word came into play with redfish because of the stout fight reds put up when hooked. There is no question about a big redfish being a "bull" to handle when taken on medium tackle.

The redfish is another of those fish that answers to a different common name as state lines are crossed. Way back in the 1950s some of the saltwater fishing members of Outdoor Writers Association of America, Inc., attempted to get a single common name recognized for each species of fish.

The common name chosen for the redfish was "channel bass." It stuck along the Atlantic Coast, but the mavericks of the Gulf Coast states would not accept it. The provincial name that stuck in the Gulf of Mexico was "redfish," or simply "red" for short. Small redfish were called "'rat reds" and those in excess of about five pounds were called "reds," while those weighing more than 20 pounds or so were referred to as "'bull reds" or simply "bulls."

There has been a move since 1980 to get "red drum" accepted as the fish's common name. This is the common name marine biologists and marine periodicals and publications use. I have a feeling it will never be universally accepted, for in journals today whenever "red drum" is used, immediately after the first use and listed in parenthesis is (redfish). The indication to me is that if you can't whip 'em, then you better look into joining them.

The full story of the redfish evolved rather slowly, and only now in the swan song year of the decade 1980 is the tale unfolding with any rapidity. Let me illustrate with some of my own research.

Back in 1970, I completed several years of considerable research on the redfish within its historic range, southward from Massachusetts to the Yucatan Peninsula on the lower Mexican Gulf Coast. The result was my fourth book for A.S. Barnes & Co., Inc. The book, *Big Red/Channel Bass Fishing,* was published in 1972.

To use a corny and time-worn phrase, a lot of water has since passed under the bridge. In the ensuing years, 1972 through 1988, great strides were made in discovering new facts about redfish. The most important was the successful spawning of redfish in hatcheries. A historic event, it made Texas the first state to bring the concept to reality. Texas continues to lead the way in the spawning and raising of redfish, mass-producing them in hatcheries and then stocking saltwater bays with the fingerlings.

Big Red/Channel Bass Fishing has been out-of-print since 1976. Consequently, some of the beliefs about redfish have changed since that book was published. That is to be expected, because fish cannot communicate with us. What we know of the individual species can only be learned by observation plus trial and error. With that thought in mind, it behooves the reader to realize that 18 years hence some of the things that appear in this edition on redfish are likely to change or be viewed in a different perspective.

But that is good, because the only way we learn is by asking questions and seeking answers.

With no more ado, let's look at *Sciaenops ocellatus,* as the fish is known scientifically, or at the "redfish," "red drum," "channel bass" or whatever provincial name is applied to the fish by the people who delight in pursuing and catching it.

By any name, the fish is truly the king of inshore saltwater gamefish along the Gulf Coast.

A.C. Becker, Jr.   Galveston, Texas

1.
THE REDFISH

The red drum, Sciaenops ocellatus, *is better known to residents of the Gulf Coast as the "redfish." The species ranges from the middle coast of Mexico northward around the entire Gulf Coast and up the Atlantic Coast to the Delaware Capes. (Photo by Larry Bozka)*

ention redfish to a fishing newcomer, and the person may conjure visions of a brick-red or fire engine-red fish. Those images are way off when it comes to the actual coloration of the redfish, or "red drum."

The coloration of this fish varies with its locality and size. The color can range from nearly white with a silver tinge to bronze or copper red. Small reds, or "rat reds," are very nearly white, particularly if they are taken from waters over hard sand or light-colored bottoms.

As the fish grow larger the coloration changes. Redfish between about five to 12 pounds generally have the most eye-appeal. Fish this size are usually a lustrous bronze to copper red, with the darker coloration along the back and upper sides. The underside of fish this size is nearly white. As redfish grow larger, particularly in the 25-pound and over range, the color ranges from overall dull silver to brassy. The underside of bull reds is a dull off-white.

The fish has a black spot at the base of the tail, and it is not unusual for a fish to have two or three spots. The additional spots are normally in line along the upper part of the body, leading from the base of the tail almost to the front of the dorsal fin.

The most spots I have seen on a redfish was 10, but I have been informed there is a specimen on record that sported 27 spots. The spot, or spots, on young redfish appear velvety-black. The redfish is a handsome, streamlined fish, more muscular but not as torpedo-shaped as members of the mackerel family. The fins have firm spines and the scales are hard and pronounced. The fish has a slightly underslung mouth, indicating that the species is basically a bottom-feeder. Its chin is fringed with small barbels that are used to pick up scent. This is important to keep in mind when one is using natural baits, as the fish can pick up scent in very sandy water.

REDFISH SIZES, MIGRATIONS

The provincial, or local name given to the redfish varies with the size of the fish and the locality in which it is found. "Redfish" or "red drum" is the common name applied to the fish found along the Gulf Coast. Those in excess of about 20 pounds are called "bull" redfish or red drum, while those weighing less than about three or four pounds are referred to as "rat" reds. Those in the range between rat reds and bull reds are simply called "redfish."

Purse seining for Gulf of Mexico redfish was outlawed in 1986, thanks in large part to an intensive letter-writing campaign conducted by concerned sportsmen. Two months after the closure, National Marine Fisheries Service biologists chartered the Mississippi-based purse seiner "Cap'n Grumpy" in order to obtain mature redfish for tagging purposes. Over 15,000 bull reds were captured, tagged and released. (Photo by Joe Richard)

The same fish found along the Atlantic Coast is most often referred to as the "channel bass," although "red drum" is often used along the lower part of the Atlantic Coast. Small specimens along most of the Atlantic Coast range are called either "puppy" red drum or red bass. In a few isolated areas, the fish is called "bar bass," "sea bass" or "redhorse." In Mexican Gulf Coast waters the fish is called "pescado colorado," which translates simply into "redfish."

At the turn of the century, the fish was believed to inhabit only the bays and surf. On the whole, the redfish was thought to be a deep-water fish.

However, studies of the fish, especially in the decades since the 1960s, have established the redfish as a species that roams offshore, both in the Gulf of Mexico and the Atlantic Ocean.

Although redfish along the Atlantic Coast are known to migrate north and south with the seasons, the species can be looked upon as being only semi-migratory along the Gulf Coast. The large specimens, the bull reds which are in fact mostly females, range in schools well offshore during most of the year. In the fall and spring they move into the surf, particularly in the vicinity of passes, cuts and channels that link the Gulf of Mexico with bays. These seasonal migrations are spawning runs. Within 24 to 48 hours after the spawn is dropped, the embryos are carried by currents into the bays. The fry immediately move into grassy areas and along the fringes of saltgrass marshes, where they find cover and sustenance until they grow large enough to forage in more open waters. Many biologists believe this happens when the small fish are about two to three inches long.

The young that escape the hazards of growing up ... loss of habitat, predators, pollution and man ... spend the next three to four years in the bays or waters in the general vicinity of where they hatched.

On occasion they temporarily move into the surf. This usually occurs when periodic freezes and abnormally low tides cause them to move out of bays and into the warmer water of the surf. When bay temperatures return to normal, the juvenile fish return to the bays.

RATE OF GROWTH

The rate of growth of redfish is reasonably fast for the first year, as the fish add an inch in length each month. The growth rate slows to about a half-inch a month during the second year, and is even slower after that. Redfish generally don't reach 30 inches ... which is about when the fish attain sexual maturity ... until four years of age. Recent studies indicate the fish can reach sexual maturity as early as three and a half years if forage and growing conditions are ideal, but most biologists believe this to be unusual.

Although small redfish less than 18 to 20 inches long are caught from the surf, most notably in the immediate vicinity of passes, cuts and channels tying the Gulf of Mexico with bays, most redfish spend the first three to four years of their lives exclusively in bays. Interesting to note is the fact that during this time span the redfish normally remain within a dozen or so miles of where the spawn was hatched.

After the redfish becomes sexually mature it spends most of the remainder of its life in the Gulf of Mexico, although it moves into the surf during the fall and spring spawning runs. The mature fish remain in schools, and rarely venture back into bays. However, you will often find 10-to 12-pound reds working bay waters, especially along the fringes of saltgrass marshes, flooded flats, and in cuts, passes and channels. Specimens of 20 pounds or more are seasonal visitors to those same passes, cuts, and channels.

Studies conducted in recent years indicate that redfish live long lives, with some still breeding at 25 to 30 years of age. Hence, protection of the breeders is very important.

The wholesale slaughter of bull redfish in the Gulf of Mexico in the 1980s took place to satisfy a new seafood rage, and seriously depleted the brood stock ... so much so that harvest quotas and maximum keeper length limits were established to protect the resource. The slaughter was made with purse seines, and the harvest during the 1980s reduced the number of brood redfish to an alarming low.

RANGE OF REDFISH

Some species of fish are found world-wide. The redfish is not one of them.

The fish is found in and native only to saltwater in the Gulf of Mexico and Atlantic Ocean. In recent years, its range has been extended to some freshwater lakes in the south, mostly in Texas, via stocking.

So far, the redfish stocked in freshwater impoundments have not reproduced. Nonetheless, some biologists feel the species will eventually adapt to the new habitat and in time will reproduce in freshwater.

At the turn of the century, the extreme saltwater range of the redfish extended from the Yucatan Peninsula on the lower Mexican Coast around the Gulf of Mexico and up the Atlantic Coast to Massachusetts. The range today is more realistically from about the middle Mexican Coast around the Gulf of Mexico and up the Atlantic Coast to the Delaware Capes.

Along with the shrinking range of the fish, the overall population is also shrinking, to the extent that every state bordering redfish waters now has conservation regulations in the form of bag limits and/or size limits. The fish has been declared a gamefish and has been removed from the commercial market in many states.

ROLE OF THE WEATHER

The weather exerts a considerable influence on this fish.

Along the Atlantic Coast, particularly to the north of Florida, redfish are migratory. They move northward to as far as the Delaware Capes during the spring and summer, and then retreat to Georgia and Florida waters in the fall and winter.

Surf and pier fishing for big redfish is a major sport along the middle range of the Atlantic Coast. Smaller reds are taken from the bays, although there is not nearly as much of this kind of fishing as is found along the Gulf Coast.

Redfish move from offshore waters and appear in the Carolina surf in the early spring. They continue to range northward as the water warms.

By the end of spring, redfish spread through Chesapeake Bay and appear in the surf from Cape Charles to Cape May. Schools of reds used to summer along the New Jersey coast, but the reduced range of the fish has made the fishing there but a shadow of what it used to be. The best and most consistent Atlantic Coast redfish action now is found during the summer along Virginia and North Carolina beaches.

Redfish taken along the Atlantic Coast are consistently larger than those caught from the Gulf of Mexico. The bulls commonly run to 50 and 60 pounds, whereas in Gulf of Mexico waters bull redfish seldom exceed 40 pounds.

Although the largest redfish appear along the Atlantic Coast, the largest population of these fish is found in the Gulf of Mexico, particularly the waters of Texas and Louisiana.

Wet and dry years play a big role in the kind of speckled trout fishing one can enjoy in a given area. The saline content of the water falls in a wet year and rises in a dry one. Speckled trout react to both variations by moving to areas where the saline content is more in keeping with their preference.

This isn't the case with redfish. Reds are much hardier than speckled trout, and they can survive in water where there may be a wide variation in salinity. Redfish seem to survive equally well in saltwater, brackish water or freshwater.

Regardless, the fish doesn't reproduce in either brackish or freshwater. This problem is being studied in redfish hatcheries, and most of this work is being done in Texas.

Small redfish are prone to move along with flood waters. They often move far into bayous, rivers and marshes on flood tides. Occasionally, on extreme flood tides, they move into depressions or cul-de-sacs that become isolated if there is an unusually fast drop in the tide. This happens most often when a tropical storm or hurricane passes over the coast. Small redfish ride with the high tides and end up in holes and depressions that under normal conditions would be miles from saltwater.

Occasionally, they survive. More often, however, they don't.

TABLE QUALITY

The greatest sport fishing pressure on redfish occurs in the Gulf of Mexico waters of Texas, Louisiana and Florida ... in that order. The primary reason is that the fish, especially the rat reds up to about 10 pounds in size, are found the year around in the numerous bays in these states.

Redfish up to about five or six pounds have always been prime choices for table fare. The meat is firm, white and tasty. Large bulls were long considered a very distant second choice because the meat is coarse and rather tasteless.

That was before the recipe for "blackened redfish" made its debut.

The Louisiana-born cooking technique transformed the meat

Length restrictions prohibit the retention of bull redfish in most Gulf states, but that doesn't negate the opportunity to mount one. This 34-incher is still swimming; the mount is an acrylic replica. Given the fish's dimensions and a quality photograph, taxidermists can create a remarkable likeness of the real thing.
(Photo by Larry Bozka)

of large redfish into a gourmet's delight, with the result being tremendous netting pressure on the vulnerable offshore breeders. Entire schools of redfish were decimated, and the overall population of these fine gamefish dropped alarmingly. Hence, ever-increasing restrictive legislation was placed on the species in the decade of the 1980s.

As far as table fare is concerned, and on a scale of one to 10, I would assign a 10 to redfish in the three-to six-or seven-pound range, a seven to the fish scaling upwards to about 15 pounds, and about a four to everything over that. That's how much I feel the quality of the meat falls off as the size of the fish increases.

Of course, the '"blackened" craze skyrockets the flesh of bulls to the nine or 10 category. But personally, I feel that with all the condiments and procedures used to achieve "blackened" status the same could be achieved with the meat from just about any species of fish.

My views of bull redfish as table fare could quite possibly be colored by experiences with big ones in my youth. I caught many of them from the mid-1930s until the late 1960s.

At first, they were fun to catch ... a big fish that didn't require the fisherman to spend a fortune on tackle or own a boat. Table-wise, the meat was really only enjoyable in fish chowder. It was too coarse and tasteless to fry, bake or broil, and back then we didn't think to mask it with a dozen spices.

Furthermore, there was nothing easy about dressing a husky 25-or 30-pound redfish. The scales were tough to remove, and the fish's bones quickly dulled even the sharpest of kitchen knives.

The bulls put up an interesting enough fight, but I gave up fishing for them when I discovered there was far more excitement in catching smaller reds ... particularly those in the five-to 12-pound range taken on the typical bay-type casting rod and reel that is so popular for speckled trout fishing. **BB**

2.
THE RIGHT TACKLE

Tackle requirements for taking redfish differ greatly from the bay to the beachfront. Reds caught out of the surf are likely to be much larger than those encountered on shallow flats. (Photo by Matt Vincent)

I remember well the first bull redfish I ever caught. My father and his cousin took me with them to fish the West Galveston Island surf on a Sunday afternoon in October. The year was 1932, and I was 12 at the time. In addition to producing my first big redfish, the trip was memorable because three bull redfish were caught at the same time.

My father and his cousin fished four rigs that afternoon. They baited each of the rigs with cut mullet. The two adults waded out about knee-deep in the surf and cast the baited hooks seaward. Then they spooled line off the reels as they backed toward the beach, where they set the rods in home-made sand spikes.

The four rods were set in a row about 25 or 30 feet apart. As was the custom in those days, the reel clickers were engaged so that the reels would make a buzzing sound when a fish picked up the bait and started swimming off with it.

At the time, none of Dad's reels had either anti-reverse dogs or star drags. You stopped line from spooling off the reel by grabbing the rod and then using your thumb to firmly press a leather tab on the reel spindle. And you wet the tab, which was called a "thumb stall," so if line was taken off very fast the friction wouldn't cause the leather to heat and blister your thumb. The trick was to slow the revolving spool enough to allow grabbing the reel handle without it beating against your knuckles.

After the baits were cast out and the rods were stuck in the sand spikes, we would go back to the car to sit on the running board and wait. When a clicker started to chatter or a reel handle began to spin, either my father or his cousin would rush out, grab the rod out of the sand spike and clamp down on the thumb stall. Carefully, they would slow the fish enough so that the reel handle could be grabbed without inflicting barked knuckles.

Under normal conditions, I never got the chance to handle a rod. My job was to string the catch on a long piece of rope and tie it off to a stake in ankle-deep water. But on that Sunday afternoon, things were different.

The reels on three of the four rods started to chatter and spin at the same time. As my father and his cousin each dashed out to grab a rod, they yelled to me to run down the beach to grab the third rig. I knew what to do from watching my father, but I had personally never before handled a big fish or a surf rig.

Somehow, I managed to press hard enough on the thumb stall to slow the spinning and grab the reel handle. I was amazed to catch it on the first try. I stopped the fish from pulling out more line, but the strain was too great for me to turn the reel handle and retrieve line. So, I did the only thing I could think of.

I started walking backward from the edge of the water.

I was back almost to the start of the sand dunes before I dragged the redfish into ankle-deep water. It was only then when I began

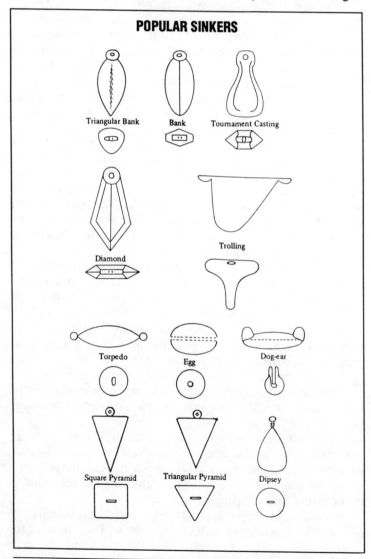

POPULAR SINKERS

Triangular Bank

Bank

Tournament Casting

Diamond

Trolling

Torpedo

Egg

Dog-ear

Square Pyramid

Triangular Pyramid

Dipsey

to crank the reel handle.

I reeled the fish, about a 20-pound bull, all the way up on the dry sand. At the time it was very exciting, and it was enough of an accomplishment for my father to brief me on what to do the next time a big redfish was hooked. He also offered that when I learned the ropes of handling the rod and reel, I could take his tackle to fish

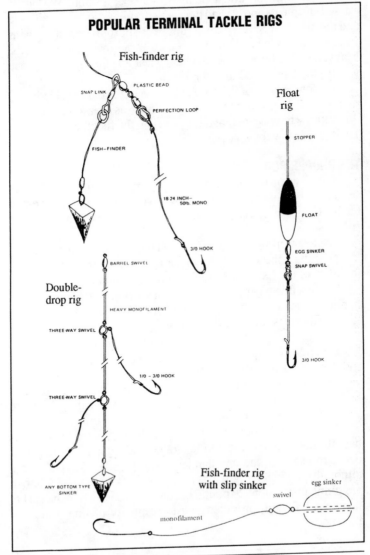

POPULAR TERMINAL TACKLE RIGS

Fish-finder rig

Float rig

Double-drop rig

Fish-finder rig with slip sinker

from the 17th Street Fishing Pier, a Galveston beachfront fishing pier that was only four city blocks from where we lived.

That was the first of many bull redfish I caught in the years that followed. In the beginning it was very exciting, but as time passed I sensed that something was missing. The ''something'' was the right tackle, but we had to forsake that for financial reasons.

This was in the midst of the Great Depression. We never missed any meals and we had two pairs of shoes ... one for daily use and the other for Sundays. But funds for appropriate fishing gear were lacking. We had to make do with home-made calcutta rods, heavy, knuckle-buster reels and heavy test line that after every trip was washed and dried to extend its life.

Just for the heck of it, I tried using one of the old knuckle-buster reels surf fishing about 15 years ago. That was a real chore. I really don't know how we managed, other than the fact that back in the 1930s redfish were very plentiful.

THE PROPER ROD

If you want to get the full enjoyment of catching redfish, including those that have to be thrown back because they are either too big or too little, it is imperative that the tackle be matched to the fish.

The fast-action bay popping rod that is so popular for speckled trout fishing is the ideal rod for catching reds in the bays, where the majority of the fish will be under about five pounds.

My first true bay popping rod was a six-foot split bamboo long-handle model. I bought it right after World War II ended, and used it until fiberglass entered the picture.

Depending upon how much you want to spend today, you can get excellent fiberglass, graphite or composite graphite-boron rods for bay fishing. The rod should be six to seven feet long so you can make long casts. Length is also important if you fish artificial lures, for by working the tip from side to side you can make a lure follow a zig-zag course in the water.

A long handle, or what some call a ''two-handed handle,'' is best for distance casting and leverage, and such a handle is less tiring to use than the one-handed pistol grip. This type of rod, although reasonably light, has sufficient backbone to handle fish weighing up to about 20 pounds. You can even use it in the surf to handle a bull red, provided you have plenty of line, time and patience.

Personally, I'm opposed to the use of such light rods in the surf, even when one is sure of beating and landing a big bull redfish. Too much time is spent fighting the fish. If the fish is above the maximum keeper length and has to be released, the odds of it surviving are very poor indeed. A fish battled to the point of exhaustion will suffer toxic shock.

Let me illustrate this with a story told to me by the late Robert Kemp, who at the time was director of fisheries for the Texas Parks and Wildlife Department.

The department, Kemp said, was seeking mature redfish to use in its hatcheries. The initial efforts were made through some Galveston-area commercial fishermen, who caught the redfish near the end of the South Jetty. They were instructed to play the fish carefully, so as not to injure them.

They did as they were asked. As a result, the fish were completely exhausted when they were landed. They suffered from shock, and failed to survive in the specially-built holding tanks.

Later, the fishermen used heavy gear and literally snatched the fish out of the water. These fish went into holding tanks in good shape and survived to become breeders for the state's saltwater stocking program.

I believe we can see a parallel in the way contestants handle largemouth bass taken during freshwater tournaments. They haul the fish out of the brush as quickly as possible. There isn't time for the fish to become exhausted. Consequently, there is a very high survival rate in bass tournaments.

If you plan to fish the surf, go with a surf rod measuring from nine to more than 11 feet long. I have a friend who uses a 14-footer. The ultimate length will depend upon what is best suited for your frame and casting ability. The length is necessary as it lets you reach above the rolling surf to make long casts ... casts that frequently must reach waters beyond the last seaward breaker.

Remember, terminal tackle (bait, sinker, etc.) that strikes the water in front of a breaking wave may be rolled closer to the beach than you intended to fish. A rolling surf packs a lot of power; just ask the people who ride surfboards. A long surf rod will give you an added advantage in turning fish when they make long runs.

If you plan to seek redfish from a pier or from a boat, where most of the fishing is in deep holes, then use a rod made for the purpose. It should be six to eight feet long and have considerable backbone.

Pier and boat rods are of about equal weight, the major difference being that pier rods are longer. Most anglers seeking redfish from piers like rods measuring nine to 11 feet long with 20- to 24-inch handles.

REELS AND LINE

Whatever kind of redfishing you want to do, the first thing to do is to select the right rod for the job. The next step is to match the reel to the rod.

An improper match can cost you both fish and enjoyment. It is easiest to make the right match by purchasing your gear from a first-class tackle shop. Unless you know what you are doing, that ''cheap buy'' at the garage sale can be a very expensive item.

There are many brands of reels on the market today. Those advertised nationally are good products. Nevertheless, a prospec-

The author has caught bull redfish as large as 38 pounds on these three reels. Using the reel on the left, he landed his first big redfish in October of 1932. The Pflueger Surf Casting model had a 1902-type drag that was controlled by four wing screws. It had no anti-reverse mechanism; instead, the fisherman had to simultaneously hold the handle and adjust the wing screws. Today, large reels have been replaced by smaller versions like those to the center and right. Line capacity, not overall size, is

tive buyer should give serious consideration to the type and brand of reel popular in the area in which he will do most of his fishing.

Reels are mechanical devices, and mechanical devices are subject to breakdowns and maintenance. There are so many brands of reels and reel sizes on the market today that many reel repair shops can't afford to stock service inventory for all of them. That, then, means there may be a time when repairs on your reel may necessitate returning it to the factory, and that could mean your reel would be out of hand for six to eight weeks. That may not mean much to a young person, but at my age that six to eight weeks is very important.

No, it pays to purchase a reel that is popular in the area, and one that can be repaired, in a manner of speaking, on the spot.

After purchasing the right rod and reel, line must be the next consideration. Line is extremely important, for it is what links you with the fish. Prior to the introduction of synthetic material line, a major problem for all fishermen was making sure the line on the reel was good.

The chore I hated most was line upkeep after every trip. I had to peel all the line off the reel, wash the line and then hang it out to dry in the shade. If you didn't take care of the line, it would rot on the reel and pop like a piece of thread.

Like the reel is matched to the rod, the line must be matched to the reel. Follow the recommendations of the reel manufacturer, but keep in mind that the heavier the line test, the less line you will be able to get on the reel.

The redfish doesn't take off line as fast as a bonefish, which can strip off 75 to 100 yards in a single blazing run. However, that doesn't mean a reduction in the line needed on the reel.

The amount of line needed on the reel will depend on the fishing. The requirements of bay fishing differ from those of surf, pier and boat fishing. Let's consider those requirements, starting with bay fishing.

Remember, back in the bays the majority of the redfish will be under five pounds. Thus, whether you use a conventional wind, open face or spincast reel, you will need one capable of holding 100 to 125 yards of eight-to 15-pound-test line. The need for pier and boat fishing will be 150 to 200 yards of 20-to 40-pound test line.

The greatest amount of line needed is in surf fishing. Go with 300 yards of 20-to 40-pound test, but bear in mind, you won't get as much casting distance when using 40-pound-test as compared to 20-pound-test.

Whatever type of reel is used, it is important to fill the spool to capacity. Doing so will make for easier casting and smoother operation of the reel's drag device. Drags always function best when the spool is filled to capacity.

LEADERS, HOOKS, SINKERS

There is really little need to use wire or cable leaders for redfish. The fish have teeth, but they are small and relatively dull. Wire or cable may be needed in waters where the bottom may be covered with sharp shells or barnacle-encrusted structure.

Twenty-pound-test monofilament is adequate for leaders used in bay fishing. Thirty-and 50-pound monofilament will serve very well as leaders for pier, boat and surf fishing. If you feel wire is necessary, use plastic-coated braided.

Most pier and boat fishermen use either fish-finder or double-drop leaders. The fish-finder rig allows the line to slip through a sinker that rests on the bottom. This is a very effective terminal rig in that it permits the current to sweep the baited hook over a considerable bottom area. The double-drop leader is one with two hook stagings above the sinker at the terminal end of the leader. This leader is used mostly by boat fishermen working channels, deep holes and along jetties.

When it comes to bay fishing, where the redfish are much smaller, the preferred terminal rig is an 18-to 24-inch leader made of 20-pound-test monofilament. The leader is attached to the line via a ringed sinker, which will hold the terminal rig in place on the bottom. The current will cause the baited hook to swing back and forth. This is an ideal and particularly effective rig to use when fishing live bait.

The hook size will depend upon where you fish. Most redfish buffs fishing in bays prefer small treble hooks, sizes No. 6 to No. 2. Single-tine hooks ranging from 2/0 to 4/0 will suffice for pier, boat and surf fishing.

Because of the size of bull redfish, some fishermen use much larger hooks. Keep in mind that it takes a lot more ''sock'' to bed a large hook in the fish's flesh. Large hooks are also easier for fish to throw, and if you're using live bait, a large hook can seriously limit the action of the bait.

One-quarter-to half-ounce ringed, rubber-core or pinch-on

(dog-ear) sinkers will serve for bay fishing. Bank or pyramid sinkers ranging from two to four ounces will suffice for pier and boat fishing. Use bank, pyramid or specially designed ''surf spider'' sinkers when fishing the surf, where sinker weight will depend on the currents and degree of surf. Go with an assortment ranging from two ounces up to six ounces.

FLOATS AND BOBBERS

Although redfish are basically bottom-feeders, there will be occasions when it will be to your advantage to keep the bait off the bottom. The most obvious times are when fishing over a bottom littered with snags or over a very soft mud bottom.

Another time is when large blue crabs are plentiful. Large bull redfish can handle the crabs, but small reds such as those found in bay fishing won't duel with big crabs for possession of a chunk of cut bait, shrimp or small baitfish. Thus, it is important to keep the bait a foot or so off the bottom. That is close enough to the bottom for foraging redfish, but high enough to be free from marauding blue crabs.

Use small floats and bobbers, especially those that don't make a lot of surface disturbance when you're reeling in. Floats will only be used in shallow water, mostly on bay flats and along the fringes of flooded saltgrass marshes. Redfish are very easy to spook, and undue manipulation of the float can often be enough disturbance to send them finning to other waters.

The popping cork may be a tremendous help in attracting speckled trout, but it is the wrong choice when trying to catch redfish in shallow water. I've had a lot of experience bolting redfish by using a noisy popping cork.

Instead of a popper, go with a float that will slide across the surface when you reel in. Also, avoid using large floats. Use just enough to suspend the bait. I prefer to use floats made of unpainted, natural cork. It has been my experience that colored floats are sometimes struck by fish.

I prefer to have fish strike the baited hook, not the float. **BB**

3.
NATURAL BAITS
FOR REDFISH

Redfish feed upon a wide variety of marine life. Studies conducted in Texas through examination of the fishes' stomach contents revealed the following combination: 40 percent shrimp, 40 percent crabs, and 20 percent mixed baitfish ... pinfish, mullet and minnows. Other food sources include squid, marine worms, barnacles and sand fiddlers. (Photo by Larry Bozka)

The best way to determine what bait to use for redfish, or for any species of fish for that matter, is to cut the fish open and examine the stomach contents. Few fishermen are willing to do this because it is rather messy. Furthermore, most fishermen are not sufficiently schooled in identifying the remains found in a fish's stomach, especially if the matter is in an advanced stage of digestion.

Studies conducted in Texas revealed the following food in redfish stomachs: 40 percent shrimp, 40 percent crabs, and 20 percent mixed fish that included pinfish, mullet and minnows.

I have never kept any percentage figures on what redfish feed upon, but in addition to the contents quoted in the Texas studies, I've found squid, marine worms, barnacles and sand fiddler remains in redfish stomachs. I've found it most interesting in that I have rarely examined a large redfish's stomach without finding the remains of blue crabs.

In the case of bull reds I've occasionally found spider crabs. Other redfish anglers tell me they, too, frequently find crab remains in the fish they catch. Yet, what is so interesting is that I have encountered very few redfish anglers who seek their fish with crabs as bait. Most prefer to use shrimp or cut bait.

Most fishermen seeking redfish base their choice of bait on where they are fishing and the size of redfish likely to be encountered. Most redfish anglers follow a rule of thumb that starts with shrimp for small reds and goes to larger baits, mainly fish species, for bull reds.

BAIT FOR BAY FISHING

Because of protective measures placed on the mature brood stock, most fishermen concentrate their efforts on reds that fall within a range of two to 12 pounds. There are no restrictions on catching bull redfish, but since in most states they are illegal to retain, the number of people purposely participating in this aspect of redfish action has dropped off drastically.

The owner of one Texas Gulf Coast fishing pier told me that when the maximum keeper length of 30 inches was placed on redfish, the business on his pier in September, October and November (the prime period for catching big redfish) dropped approximately 70 percent.

Fishing pressure on small redfish has increased over the years because of the maximum length regulation as well as the fact that

Blue crabs are a regular part of the redfish's diet. Yet, few fishermen use them as bait. Small crabs measuring four to five inches across the carapace can be fished whole, but larger specimens should be shelled and halved. The blue crab is an excellent choice for fishing the surf or deep holes adjacent to jetties. (Photo by A.C. Becker, Jr.)

the meat of small reds is vastly superior to that of the large bulls. There is no point in listing the minimum keeper length in this book, because it varies from state to state and is altered every few years.

The situation is the same with the maximum keeper length as well as the daily bag and possession limits. Each of the regulations is subject to change with the fluctuation of the redfish population.

The optimists believe the restrictions will eventually be liberalized. I'm inclined to believe otherwise. There is heavy sport and commercial fishing pressure on the redfish, and I don't expect to see it lessen.

The most effective bait for small redfish, those up to about three or four pounds, is the live shrimp. If live shrimp are not available, a good second choice is fresh dead shrimp.

If the dead shrimp are large, break each into two chunks. Be sure to peel the tail portion. Insert the bait on the hook by running it lengthwise over the point and up the shank until the point pokes free of the bait. Leave the head on the front portion if the shrimp is fresh, but discard it if the head has started to turn black or has a foul odor.

If live shrimp are used, place the bait on the hook in the same manner as when fishing for speckled trout. Small live shrimp can be hooked through the second section of the body from the tail. Larger shrimp can be hooked under the spike atop the shrimp's head.

If the area you are fishing has a soft, muddy bottom, fish the live shrimp suspended under a float that will keep the bait a few inches above the bottom. If a live shrimp is allowed to settle on the bottom, it will often burrow into the mud to escape predators. Of course, you won't have this problem when fishing dead shrimp on the bottom.

Small live mullet and mud minnows three to four inches long make excellent redfish baits for working the edges of saltgrass marshes, around flooded grass stands and on shallow flats where the bottom is reasonably hard sand. Use these baits with a fish-finder type terminal rig.

Large mullet or small panfish can be filleted and cut into chunks for cut bait. When placed on the hook, be certain the point protrudes out of the meat and will therefore be able to bed in the fish's mouth. Be sure, too, to always use fresh mullet and panfish for bait.

If small blue crabs are available, break off the pincher claws and insert the hook through one of the claw sockets on the crab's body. Again, make certain the point and barb of the hook is free of the body.

It helps to crack or partially crush the crab's carapace. The juices that ooze out make an effective chum slick. This is a good way to fish for redfish when the water is off-color. Remember those barbels on the fish's chin; they will pick up the scent.

As redfish grow larger, they turn more to small fish as the staple in their diet. If you're fishing an area where you know the reds will be in the six-to 12-pound range, go with fresh cut bait. An eight-to 10-inch mullet cut into two pieces is excellent. Most anglers using these baits prefer to cut the mullet diagonally.

The head portion is put on the hook by running the hook through both lips. The tail portion is hooked through the opening, with the point and barb run out of the underbelly. Don't bother to clean out the cavity exposed by the cut. Like the aforementioned crab, the mullet oozes fluids that will cause a thin chum slick. Here again is that appeal to the fish's sense of smell ... a factor that's extremely important when seeking redfish.

SURF BAITS FOR REDFISH

Baits for surf fishing must be much sturdier than those for bay fishing. The baits must be firm and hard enough to withstand the rigors of long casts, a pounding surf and often very strong currents.

Large dead shrimp can be used in the fall when the water is cool enough to make scavengers scarce. Place the shrimp whole on the hook. Insert the hook into the underside and near the tail of the shrimp. Work the shrimp up the shank of the hook and make sure the point and barb protrude out of the underside of the shrimp, near its head. If it's fresh, leave the head on the shrimp so that it will ooze fluid. Discard the head if it is very mushy and is beginning to turn black. Decaying shrimp or any bait with a vile odor will only attract scavengers. Redfish, like most gamefish, go for fresh bait.

Forget about trying to use live shrimp for surf fishing. The force needed to make long casts will snap the shrimp off the hook. If the shrimp should still be on the hook after the cast, it will not be

Squid makes a great bait for surf fishing, primarily because it is leather-tough and will therefore withstand the rigors of pounding waves. Equally important, the fisherman can put power into the cast without fear of snapping the bait off the hook. (Photo by Larry Bozka)

there long because of the pounding surf and strong currents.

Since the majority of the redfish in the surf will run from about 10 or 12 pounds up, use large chunks of cut bait. Again, cut the mullet or panfish in half diagonally, and bait the hook in the same manner as when fishing the bays.

Live mullet, six to eight inches long, can be used in the surf. Hook the mullet through the body just ahead of the tail or through both lips. When hooking through the lips, exercise care on the cast so as not to snap the bait off the hook.

Blue crabs make excellent baits for working the surf. A crab with a four-to five-inch carapace can be used whole. Break off the pincher claws and insert the hook through one of the sockets on the body, taking care to work the hook around so that both the point and barb are exposed. If you don't, the hard carapace could interfere with the hook biting into the flesh of the fish. Again, crack or partially crush the carapace so body fluids will leak out.

Another good choice for surf fishing is squid. This is a tough bait that is hard to tear off the hook. You can put power into your casts for distance and you won't snap squid off the hook. Squid will also withstand the rigors of the pounding surf. Be sure, however, that the hook point protrudes out of the squid.

BAIT FOR PIER, BOAT FISHING

Whether one uses shrimp, small live fish or cut bait when seeking redfish from boats or piers depends on the time of the year.

Large bull shrimp, the kind that run 10 to 12 to the pound, are excellent for fall and winter fishing, when the water is cold enough to send the scavengers and bait-stealers into hiding. During the spring, summer and early fall live mullet, small panfish and cut bait will prompt the most action. Large live shrimp will appeal to redfish in the warm-weather months, but there will be that problem of losing a lot of them to scavengers and blue crabs. As a result, you can end up spending more time re-baiting the hooks than fishing.

In spite of the fact that blue crabs make up a considerable part of a redfish's diet, not many fishermen use crabs for bait. I find this unusual because so many of the people who fish for large black drum, a poorer cousin of the redfish, lean heavily to crabs when fishing during the black drum run. That run generally occurs at the tail end of winter and covers the first two months of spring.

I have had notable success catching big redfish on crabs when

A quality castnet is good insurance when the need arises for live bait. Smaller nets in the three-and-a-half-foot size range are far easier to throw than larger versioins, epecially for the beginner. (Photo by A.C. Becker, Jr.)

fishing from boats around jetties, in deep channels or from piers along the beachfront. When using a crab with a four-to five-inch carapace, I break off the pincher claws and fish the crustacean live. However, I do crack the carapace for additional scent.

When no small crabs are available, I use large blue crabs. With these, pull off the carapace and then break the body in half to make two baits. I neither clean out the cavity nor remove the grayish-colored muscle matter found between the carapace and the body. I remove the pincher claws, but leave the fingers attached to the body. The current will cause the fingers to move, and I feel this helps in attracting the fish by sight.

Once again, the fluids that seep out of the body cavity and the scent of the muscle matter help the redfish locate the bait. I don't think you can over-emphasize the importance of scent when redfish are the target.

In respect to scent, I feel a lot can be said for the fish attractants on the market today. If nothing more, these scents will cover human odors. But I feel there is more to the attractants than that. The problem appears to be that most fishermen use them improperly. The scents need to be used in an area long enough for a scent line to be established. A half-dozen casts with fish scent on the bait won't accomplish much if you keep moving to new areas. **BB**

4.
CATCHING REDFISH ON LURES

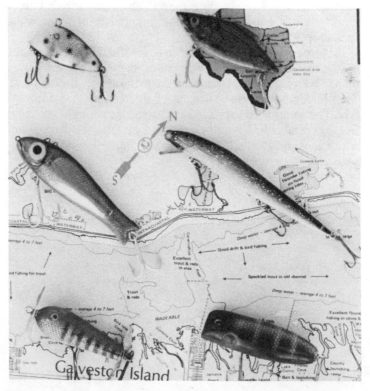

Plugs for redfishing should be selected in accordance with the water to be fished. Long-lipped divers can be deadly on clear-water sand flats, especially when the target is tailing redfish. Torpedo-shaped plugs are effective when drift fishing the bays and wading the surf. (Photo by A.C. Becker, Jr.)

've caught a lot of redfish on artificial lures: plugs, spoons, bait-tails, jigs and flies. The vast majority of those taken on lures ranged up to about 10 to 12 pounds. Although I've caught a lot of bull reds, relatively few were taken on artificial lures.

I don't know that I could call my artificial lure experience with bull redfish typical, however, because I stopped fishing specifically for the big ones back in the middle 1960s. As far as I am concerned, the redfish in the five-to 10-or 12-pound range are more sporting to catch. They are bay fish, and I prefer to fish in bays rather than the surf or from a pier. Redfish in the weight range mentioned wage a more interesting fight, and they are far better table fare than the big bulls.

There is also the thrill of seeing the water boil or watching V-shaped wakes crease the surface as a hooked fish surges over shallow-water flats.

There is a big difference in how redfish respond to artificial lures. When the schools are large, small redfish often hit with reckless abandon ... so much so, in fact, that it can cause a newcomer to have doubts about the stories of redfish being curious fish and easy to spook.

Larger reds in the five-to 12-pound range readily take lures, but they don't respond to being hooked as quickly as the small ones. The small reds hit harder and more suddenly, and they wage an aggressive fight. The larger ones, those in the five-to 12-pound range, are more likely to grab the lure, turn away and not respond to the hook until they feel the point bite deep into their flesh. At that point, they can make the water on a shallow flat storm-like.

Big bull redfish seem to be even slower in responding. I've had big ones pick up a lure and leisurely swim off with it but not respond until I struck a couple or three times to bed the hook. They make a strong run, but not the sudden takeoff of smaller specimens.

FISHING SPOONS

Half-ounce-to three-quarter-ounce spoons ... silver or gold and usually adorned with a red, white or yellow skirt or bucktail ... are deadly for seeking redfish in the bays. On the flats and along the fringes of flooded saltgrass stands and marshes, the fluttering metal baits are especially potent.

There is no set, one-way-only method of working spoons for

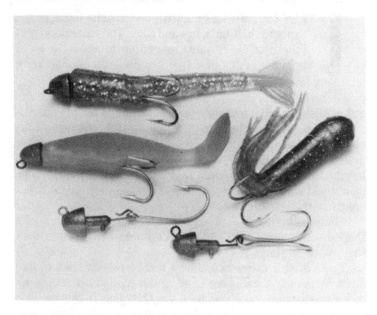

The development of the Flex-Jig, a new concept in lead-head jigs, expanded the use of soft plastic bait-tail lures. The Flex-Jig is adaptable for use with single, double or treble hooks, and can be used with a wide assortment of bait-tails. The Flex-Jig concept allows a flexible range of motion between the jig head and the hook, and as such makes it much more diffiicult fot the fish to throw.

reds. What pays off one day may turn out to be a curse the next day. As a matter of fact, I have experienced drastic changes in a matter of hours. Why the changes, I don't know. All you can really do is to keep experimenting until you start catching fish or getting strikes. Stick with that technique until the action stops, and then start experimenting again.

Fishing with a spoon can be most challenging. The spoon is certainly the artificial lure to use if the water is a bit sandy or off-color. The flash of a wobbling spoon can be seen in lightly off-colored water if the water is shallow and the spoon is worked close enough to the surface to catch light.

A spoon is an excellent lure to use when fishing the flats, and it can be particularly deadly when redfish are working in schools. This is when schooling fish may even compete for the lure. I have never experienced it, but I know several waders who have experienced catching two redfish at the same time on the same spoon.

The spoon is very effective when a fisherman is working tailing redfish. This is when the fish are rooting the bottom, in water so shallow that their tails stick above the surface of the water. This is a situation where you have to fish with the utmost caution, because tailing reds will spook almost at the drop of a hat.

A second "best time" for spoons is in the winter, when cold temperatures cause the redfish to school on the bottom of deep holes, channels and cul-de-sacs. The spoons, however, should be relatively small, no more than about three inches. Attach a No. 6 or No. 8 treble hook to the spoon and hide it in a white or yellow bucktail or skirt. Clip the skirt or bucktail short so that just the points of the hook show.

Remember, fish are cold-blooded creatures that take on the temperature of the element in which they live. The colder the water, the more sluggish the fish become. Instead of grabbing their food, they tap at it. This is a situation where a small hook pays the biggest dividends, not in size of fish but rather in numbers.

The most productive technique to use in cold weather is to let the spoon hit the bottom, dip the rod tip toward the water and then lift the rod tip straight up. Wiggle the rod tip, then quickly dip the tip back to the surface of the water. Do this fast enough so the spoon will seem to be falling free. Most of the redfish pickups will occur when the spoon is tumbling back toward the bottom.

Spoons are good lures to use in the spring and summer, when redfish in the seven-to 12-pound range often work around jetties and in the passes that connect bays with the Gulf of Mexico. Usually these are redfish making their first foray into the Gulf of Mexico. Good catches can be made by jigging large spoons, five-to seven-inch models, in deep holes along jetties or along the stepoff on channels and cuts in the spring and summer.

PLUGGING FOR REDFISH

The most productive way to fish plugs is to work them deep and along the bottom. The retrieve should be only moderate, because redfish usually don't go charging after fast-moving baits unless they are quite small and are working in big schools. Save the fast plug retrieve for speckled trout.

The plug can be either a torpedo-shaped fast sinker or a floater with a large lip that will cause it to dive when retrieved. The long-lipped floater-diver is a deadly plug for fishing shallow water flats at night and along the edges of saltgrass marshes on extremely high tides. If there are open-water paths leading back into the marsh, try fishing the floater-divers there.

The approach to this kind of plugging must be stealthy, because the fish can be skittish and will spook at the slightest unusual noise or commotion. When redfish spook, they may move to waters several hundred yards away. Speckled trout spook, too, but they usually move only a few yards before they settle down.

The torpedo-shaped plugs are good for fishing the surf when the water is reasonably clear and for drift-fishing in bays. The ability to make long casts is a must when fishing the bays. That holds for both wade fishing and drift fishing. Along with distance, you need reasonably good accuracy, although not as pin-point as is necessary when seeking largemouth bass in freshwater.

Plugging for redfish in bays calls for one to have the ability to read the water. Watch the surface of the water for baitfish activity. Work to within casting range and plunk the plug into the water just

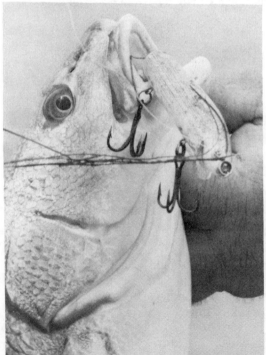

The broken-back topwater plug is a favorite of flats fishermen, especially those who frequent Texas' Laguna Madre. Also called "crippled-minnows," the jointed baits convincingly imitate the motion of wounded baitfish. (Photo by Larry Bozka)

ahead of the direction in which the bait is moving.

If the water is very shallow, drop the plug immediately behind the baitfish. Work the plug in short jerks to create the impression of a crippled minnow. Always look for small patches of sandy water. Frequently, those patches are caused by schools of redfish rooting the bottom. Work the plugs along the edges of the sandy water.

The long-lipped diver can be a lethal lure on sand flats when the water is clear. Redfish are basically bottom-feeders, and they are quite like their cousins, the black drum, in that they will nose along the bottom to uproot marine worms. A school of redfish working an area in this manner can create a lot of small depressions on the bottom.

The depressions are similar to those caused by grubbing black drum, but they are not nearly as large in diameter or depth.

If redfish are seen tailing, cast the diver plug ahead of the fish and work it on a collision course with the fish or school of fish. Get the plug down on the bottom and reel it just fast enough to cause the long lip to walk along the bottom. This will cause a sand streak in the water, and it is very much like the streak caused by a blue crab scurrying rapidly along the bottom.

I've worked these bottom-bumping plugs in water 18 to 24 inches deep and had redfish turn and follow the sandy streak to its source. For this kind of plugging, I like a green-backed diver with diagonal light stripes on its sides. This is a fair imitation of a small blue crab.

Why a green back for a blue crab? That's the color of the carapace of small blue crabs. The shells darken to greenish-blue as the creatures age and grow larger.

Floaters that dive and run shallow on retrieve are effective when working shallow water along the edges of saltgrass marshes. Again, a good finish is green with light diagonal stripes. On a slow retrieve and moving along about six inches below the surface, the plug is a good imitation of a swimming blue crab.

Broken-back plugs, or what we used to call ''jointed'' plugs, are also good choices for this kind of fishing. I've used plugs crafted exactly like small blue crabs, but have had very limited success.

BAIT-TAILING FOR REDS
And then there's that old adage about saving the best for last.

That's exactly what I've done in respect to the lead-head soft-tailed lures popularly called bait-tails, shrimp-tails or minnow-tails.

The head of this lure is made of lead, and usually is painted white, red, yellow or black with an eye on each side. The lead is cast on a single, long-shanked hook which in turn is inserted into a soft plastic shrimp, minnow or worm.

The weighted head makes for easy distance casting. The soft tail wiggles seductively when the lure is retrieved, and the softness of the tail gives it a feel of realness when it is mouthed by a fish.

Fish that hit hard-bodied lures but fail to get hooked usually don't return for a second try. The thing they bumped just didn't feel real.

Not so with bait-tails.

The tail is as soft and pliable as the creature it is meant to imitate. Hence, fish will hit again and again at the lure. This isn't bait manufacturer talk. Many fishermen have experienced or reported seeing the same fish strike time after time at soft-bodied lures.

As far as artificial lure fishing is concerned along the Texas coast, the bait-tail has become the No. 1 fish-taker. The lure is very easy to use, and its weight and shape allow it to be cast the proverbial "country mile." What makes the bait-tail even more acceptable is the price. You can buy a half-dozen or so for the price of one good spoon or plug.

POPULAR BRANDS

I have avoided mentioning brand names on purpose. When you consider the entire range of the redfish from the middle Mexican Gulf Coast to the Delaware Capes, a lure that is popular along one stretch of the coast may be unknown on other sections.

A lure is a "best" choice in one area and an unknown in another because of the fishermen themselves. I found it an education doing research for my book *Lure Fishing* (A.S. Barnes & Co., Inc., 1970). First off, fishermen and not fish determine the colors and finishes manufacturers put on their products. The name of the game is "You have to catch the fisherman first."

So he is caught. What next?

If he catches fish on the lure and his friends learn about it, they beat a path to the tackle shop. If they, too, catch fish, the story is repeated many times, and soon that particular lure becomes a

Of all the artificial lures available to today's coastal fishermen, the lead-headed bait-tail is the all-around favorite. The baits are inexpensive, cast long distances with a minimum of effort and, best of all, and are as soft and natural-feeling as the crustaceans they imitate. (Photo by Larry Bozka)

byword in the area. If the first purchaser failed to catch fish on the product, the lure most likely will go into the ''dead letter file,'' a catch-all for unneeded items in the fellow's garage, shop room or attic. If the item is ever resurrected, it will probably be for a garage sale.

Lures live and die on the whims of the people who buy and fish them. That's the reason some lure manufacturers make special concessions to entice guides and professionals to use their products.

I have long contended that if you give a couple of hundred fishermen the same lure and offer some worthwhile prizes for the biggest or most fish caught on the lures in three days, you will quickly popularize the brand used. What it gets down to is fishermen make a brand or finish popular. Thus, the manufacturer with the best distribution system is the one whose lures will be the most popular. **BB**

5.
REDFISH IN
THE BAYS

Shallow-water bay fishing should be timed to coincide with the incoming tide. The rising water inundates new bottom areas which in turn offer feeding redfish an easy meal. Reds weighing up to 10 or 12 pounds will move into water that measures a mere 18 inches deep. (Photo by Larry Bozka)

Maximum length limits prohibiting the retention of bull redfish have made a marked change in the fishing for this fine gamefish. When large redfish were legal to keep, the bulk of the fishing for reds was in the surf and in the deep holes along channels and passes, around the ends of jetties and particularly from beachfront fishing piers. This kind of fishing was heaviest during the spring and summer along the Middle Atlantic Coast, and in the spring and fall along the Gulf Coast states.

Surf and deep hole fishing are still the most popular techniques along the Atlantic Coast range of the redfish from northern Georgia to the Delaware Capes. The picture is different, however, in the Gulf Coast states, where the main play for redfish now is in the bays.

There are many ways to fish for redfish in bays: around grass stands, on the flats, around reefs, in tidal bayous, and along the bay side of passes and cuts. Each requires a variation in the approach and technique.

FISHING GRASS STANDS

One of the surest ways to find redfish in the bays is to concentrate your efforts along the fringes of saltgrass marshes and around grass stands. These are areas where bait is concentrated.

Time your fishing to coincide with the incoming tide. Years ago, the old salts used to say the best time for redfish was in a period that ranged from about two hours before the high tide stand until about two hours after the tide turned and began to fall. Along the Texas Coast, this has become known as the "two-plus-two rule."

Down through the years the rule has been extended to cover just about all species of bottom-feeding inshore fish. The reason should be obvious; the rising tide covers new bottom areas that open additional feeding areas to the fish.

On a normal tide look for the redfish action to occur along the edges of saltgrass marshes. The action is generally the best when the "two-plus-two" tide rule coincides with low light conditions. This means at night, early in the morning or under a very heavy overcast.

I've found that a light rain or drizzle is a big help in this kind of fishing. Perhaps the dappling of raindrops on the surface of the water stimulates the fish. If nothing else, the patter of raindrops on the surface may screen out some of the noise made by approaching fishermen.

If the high tide is unusually high and raises the water level to the point where only the tips of the grass stand clear, look for redfish to work right in the grass. They seem to love to feed on the small marine life that attaches to the grass. Artificial lures are difficult to fish in the grass, unless you use a bait-tail and then rig the tail to cover the hook point to prevent it from fouling in the grass.

A far better option for this kind of fishing is to go with natural bait, either live or cut. You can often see the redfish working through the grass. Just watch for unusual movement of the grass sticking above the surface and then cast the bait toward where the fish appear to be moving.

The most effective way to work the edge of the marshes is to wade fish. You can move along with very little noise, and if you move carefully you can keep right up with the fish. You can drift fish in a boat, if the wind blows parallel to the edge of the marsh. The smaller the boat and the dingier its finish the better.

That gleaming white boat isn't for shallow water fishing.

If you do want to drift fish, make a careful approach and cut off the engine a good hundred yards or so from the marsh. Then pole the boat into casting range. Don't use oars or paddles; they make too much noise.

FISHING BAY FLATS

Fishing for redfish on bay flats is exciting and dramatic, and at times much like bonefishing in that you actually see and stalk the fish.

Fishing the flats is best on the high tide, when flooding water opens new avenues for fish to feed. Often the water may be only about a foot and a half deep, yet reds up to 10 and 12 pounds will prowl over these flats.

This is when you are most likely to see redfish "tailing." This occurs when the fish slowly cruise nose-down in shallow water to root the bottom. Sometimes when they are standing on their noses, their tails will wave above the surface. The thrill is supreme when you see a tailing red, cast just ahead of the fish and then have the fish grab the bait or lure.

Fishing the flats isn't easy. Generally, the water is too shallow for drifting in a boat, so it means getting out and wading. A problem in wade fishing in shallow water is the tendency to move too quickly. You don't want to make any noise or any waves that may spook the fish.

Artificial lures are excellent for fishing the flats. If you prefer to use natural bait, go with live shrimp, small mullet or mud minnows.

If you are skilled in accurate distance casting with fly tackle, seeking reds on the flats can be your cup of tea. Wet flies and tiny spinners are best. Lay them in the water just ahead of tailing redfish or patches of "nervous water." This is the term old salts use to describe the surface of the water when baitfish are fidgety and are being herded by gamefish.

FISHING BAYOUS, CUTS

Fine redfish action can be enjoyed in the bayous and cuts that wind through the marshes or into the prairies that border bays. The best fishing in these waters is in the spring and summer and on the high tide. How well one scores usually depends upon correlating where one fishes with the stage of the tide.

Do your fishing well into the bayous and cuts on the rising tide

Redfish feeding in super-shallow water are extremely skittish. Wade fishing, therefore, is the best way to go when approaching these fish. In such a situation, the ability to make accurate casts plays a critical role. (Photo by Larry Bozka)

43

and high tide stand, but confine your attention to the mouths when the tide turns and begins to fall. Don't look for big redfish, because bayous are not their territory. In fact, most of the redfish found in these waters are specimens under about three pounds, and if you fish in a state with a minimum keeper length on redfish you may have to skip these waters completely or be satisfied with throwing back every red you catch.

Furthermore, the bulk of this fishing will have to be with natural bait, either live or cut, for the simple reason that the water in these bayous and cuts is usually too off-color for the use of artificial lures.

If you must use artificials, go with spoons. They are the easiest to see when the water is sandy.

When the tide is rising or at full high, you can get into good fishing in bayous and cuts as far back as the headwaters. Fish the mouth or just outside the mouth when the tide begins to fall.

Fishing the mouth of a bayou can often be excellent during the first hour or two of a falling tide. Redfish seem to start out all at the same time on the falling tide, but the action is usually confined to only an hour or two. After that, the redfish may be few and far between.

Specific areas to fish in bayous and cuts are around small islets, the outside fringes of turns, reefs, and coves and the mouths of finger bayous that extend offshore from the main waterway.

FISHING HOLES AND CHANNELS

If you plan to do winter fishing in bays, you must know the locations of deep holes and dead-end channels. These are the waters redfish retreat to when the water temperature drops or when tides fall abnormally low, as is often the case when weather fronts are accompanied by strong northerly winds.

Winds that herald in winter weather fronts have a dramatic effect on the water level in Gulf Coast bays, especially along the western Gulf of Mexico. Water levels in bays on the Atlantic Coast are less critical because the bays are generally deeper than those of the Gulf Coast. Water level drops of three feet below the predicted height for the low tide stand are common during the winter along the eastern Gulf Coast.

Old salts say the strong northerly winds simply "blow the water out of the bays." The opposite of "blowing the water out of the bays" occurs with strong and sustained easterly winds that cause tides to rise much higher than predicted in the bays along the western Gulf of Mexico. Strong southerly winds have the same effect on bays of the northern Gulf Coast.

Redfish respond more to rising and falling water in bays than do most other species of inshore gamefish. This is a common characteristic of bottom-feeding fish.

Consequently, when a low tide occurs during the warm months, the redfish retreat to the fringes of holes and along the edges of channels. This also occurs during the winter months; only then, there are two reasons for the reds to go to deep water.

Obviously, the first is the lack of water on the flats. The other is for relief from the cold.

Fish are cold-blooded creatures. Their bodies assume the temperature of the water in which they live, and their food intake is directly associated with the temperature. The colder the water, the slower the metabolism of the fish and the less they feed. The fish become very sluggish in cold water, and move into deep areas where the water temperature is more stable.

The holes and dead-end channels are the areas to fish in the winter. Particularly good are those where currents are negligible. Fish the bottom and along the bottom edge of the stepoffs and slopes. Work the bait or lure slowly, and don't expect the fish to strike hard. The hits will be more like taps than definite pickups.

FISHING POINTS, REEFS

A lot of people who seek redfish in bays like to fish a particular point or reef. They wait for the fish to come to them rather than move around, wading or drifting in a boat to find fish. It is a stationary way to fish, and is usually much slower than either wade fishing or drift fishing.

The key is to find the places redfish frequent or areas where they school. The most likely areas, given the normal range of tides, are off points that finger out into the bay and around live oyster reefs. Small marine life is generally plentiful in the vicinity of points. Most will be found on the side protected from the wind.

Redfish readily move up and down oyster reefs, feeding on the life that gathers around the shells. The best action is mainly along the side of the reef where the water is deepest. A good place to fish is at the point of a reef.

Use natural bait, either live or cut, when fishing a point or a reef. You can resort to artificial lures if you get into a school of

Fishing under the lights is a very effective way to fish canals and bayous that feed into bays. Concentrate your efforts near small islets and the outside fringes of reefs and coves. (Photo by A.C. Becker, Jr.)

reds, but redfish really aren't that plentiful anymore. I remember fishing trips 30 to 40 years ago when I threw spoons and caught several dozen rat reds without having to move more than a dozen feet from where I started. But that was when redfish were extremely plentiful and before bag limits and minimum size limits were adopted.

Today, when fishing a point or a reef you will do much better using natural bait. The scent will help to attract fish, especially if there is enough of a scent to cause a chum line or slick.

In this respect I have found that fish attractants offer the so-called "still fisherman" a definite advantage. Carried by the current, it will cause a scent slick. This is very effective, because redfish are primarily scent feeders.

EFFECTS OF RAINFALL

Either the lack of rainfall or excessive amounts of rain can make drastic changes in bay fishing for most species of gamefish. The redfish, however, is one of the least influenced.

The red seems to be equally at home in very salty water as in brackish and freshwater. The only difference noted in redfish is that they do not reproduce in brackish or freshwater.

Redfish in bays seem inclined to feed more readily in moderately salty areas. As an example, consider where redfish range during a wet season when there is a lot of freshwater runoff into a bay. They will invariably be caught deep along the edges of channels and holes rather than on shallow flats.

I have experienced many occasions when some of the people in my group fished under floats while others fished deep. During excessive freshwater runoff periods, when the surface water was almost "sweet" enough to drink, those who fished under a float caught no redfish. Those who fished the identical waters at the same time but who worked their baits nearer the bottom caught redfish. I suspect the redfish stayed deep because that was where the bait moved in response to the fresh surface water. Had the bait remained high in the freshwater, I feel the redfish would have been there, too. **BB**

6.
REDFISH IN THE SURF

Increased fishing pressure on redfish populations throughout the 1980s prompted most coastal states to enact maximum size restrictions on the species. Fish like this one taken from the surf at Third Pass, Mexico, nonetheless continue to offer exciting catch-and-release action to beachfront fishermen. Those fishermen, however, should take every precaution to avoid injury to the fish. (Photo by Larry Bozka)

here was an era when a good percentage of redfishing was done in the surf. That changed when maximum length limits were placed on the fish in many states.

No restrictions were placed on catching big redfish, provided they were immediately released. The purpose of the maximum length rule is to protect the brood stock. Under normal conditions, redfish don't breed until they are about four years old and longer than 28 to 30 inches.

Not only are the fish late breeders, but almost all redfish in excess of 30 inches are females. Male redfish rarely live longer than five to seven years, whereas the females often reach 20 to 30 years of age.

With restrictions on keeping big redfish, there is far less fishing pressure on the big specimens. There is a move in some states to allow the retention of one bull redfish per year, and there is even talk about a fishing license with a redfish tag attached, much like hunting licenses have deer tags attached.

THE BEST TIME, TIDES

Even though it is illegal to keep bull redfish in many states, there are still a number of fishermen who just want to say they caught a big one. It is with this in mind that this chapter is written. Read it, but keep in mind that the fish must be immediately returned to the water.

There are two "best times" to fish the surf for reds. Both coincide with spawning runs, with the major run occurring in the fall. It generally starts in September and continues into December. The second run is less dramatic, and it extends from late March through April.

The best time can even be broken down from the season to the day. So many big redfish are caught at night or under very poor light conditions that one sometimes considers the big ones to be nocturnal. Since these are spawning runs, when the fish move into the surf, the fact that most of the fish show up at night may be Mother Nature's twist in protecting the species.

The height of the tide will determine where one should fish the surf. When the tide is high, the fish often move into the second trough from the beach. On an extremely high tide they sometimes move into the first seaward trough, where I've caught 20-to 25-pound bulls from water only about two feet deep. When the tide is

low, the best fishing is usually just beyond the third seaward sand bar.

Surf fishing for redfish can be enjoyed anywhere in the range of the fish, meaning from the Delaware Capes to the middle Mexican Coast. The best fishing always occurs in the vicinity of passes, cuts and channels that link the open sea with bays, and it is particularly good in the surf that pounds the beaches of barrier islands.

The spawning run that occurs along the Gulf Coast in September can be triggered to start as early as the second week in August.

The circle hook, also known as the "tuna hook," is made-to-order for both surf-running redfish and conservation-conscious beachfront anglers. The circular design of the shank and point eliminates the possibility of a throat-hooked fish. When the fish strikes the bait, the angular barb curves into its jaw. The hookset is virtually automatic. (Photos by Larry Bozka)

The "trigger" is invariably a tropical disturbance that may go from just that, a tropical disturbance, right up to a full-blown hurricane. Blows that roll ashore after the second week in August are almost always followed by a major bull redfish surf run that starts about 24 hours after the blow passes inland. I vividly recall my father and his friends eagerly looking forward to surf fishing the day after a blow piled ashore on the Texas coast or ran parallel to the coast and then went inland in Louisiana.

The most graphic surf run I personally experienced occurred in the early 1960s, right after a hurricane passed just off the Texas coast and slammed into Louisiana. By actual count, more than 6,000 bull redfish weighing 25 pounds or more were caught from the Galveston Island surf and beachfront piers in one week. I was writing daily fishing news for the *Galveston Daily News* at the time, and I had people calling with reports of as many as a dozen big reds per day. Reporting the catches in the newspaper reached a fever pitch.

I have often wondered how many unreported big redfish were caught in that same week. It was a horrible waste of the resource, but at the time very few people, including the writer, realized it. There was still that lingering belief that the world's oceans and seas were too vast to ever be depleted of marine life.

READING THE SURF

Successful surf fishing for redfish depends upon reading the surf and interpreting water conditions as to where to fish.

The starter is to always fish in the vicinity of a pass or cut linking the open sea with a bay. The best fishing is often directly

Timing and proper technique are essential to surf casting. The principle parallels a golf swing. Body weight is shifted from one foot to the other, and your body pivots as the cast is made. Follow-through continues until the rod tip is pointed toward the target area. (Photo by Larry Bozka)

within the cut or pass, but ''vicinity'' can also mean the surf 25 or so miles to either side of the sea-bay connection.

The condition most fishermen desire is that of clear water. This is fine for seeking fish that depend heavily on sight for their food, but this is not the right water for surf anglers seeking redfish. Big redfish are extremely easy to spook in clear water.

Mild to reasonably sandy water is what the surf fisherman wants. This will hide the fisherman, who has to wade out to cast for the fish. The suspended sand also will cause a lot of small marine life to come out of hiding. That, in turn, will attract larger marine life and go right on up the ladder to bull redfish. The ideal condition is where the water out beyond the third seaward bar is reasonably clear, with the water becoming increasingly sandy as one moves nearer to the beach. Clear water is fine, in fact excellent, for speckled trout ... but not for redfish.

A surf with about three to four lines of breakers is best. Wherever a wave breaks it churns the bottom and breaks free marine life, and in effect opens the food trough for scent-and bottom-feeding fish. The redfish happens to be both. You want to place your baited hook (lures are poor for sandy water) in this curtain of sandy water.

READING THE BEACH

In addition to reading the surf, learn how to read the beach. This will help to determine where you should fish and how far out to cast. You can find good places by standing at the edge of the water and looking down the shoreline, not just a few hundred feet but a quarter-to a half-mile or so. Note how the shoreline gently scallops, alternating gentle inward curves with equally gentle points. These are formed by the surf and currents, and conform with the general shape of the bottom immediately offshore.

The gentle inward curves are indicative of cuts across the sand bars just out from the beach. Cast your bait into or near these cuts across the bars, because these are the areas where fish move back and forth from trough to trough.

Search the shoreline for patches of shell. These indicate the presence of nearby offshore shell patches. Dig down into the shell patches and note the amount of small marine life ... an all-important element in the food chain of redfish.

You will occasionally find muddy areas on the beach. Pay attention to them, and try the adjacent waters. Offshore, there will be similar muddy areas. Muddy bottoms are usually rich with marine worms, and marine worms are readily taken by redfish.

HOW TO SURF CAST

Surf casting is an art, and it is an art that not everyone can perform with satisfaction and skill. The correct gear is only the starter.

Select surf gear with care, making sure all components balance in the overall picture. After that, proper casting and being able to plunk the baited hook at the targeted spot is a matter of good coordination and timing. The length of the rod and weight of the baited terminal gear dictates that the cast has to be made with two hands. The cast is almost like driving a golf ball, in that the entire body comes into play. Your weight is shifted from one foot to the other, your body pivots and you execute a high, graceful arc with both arms. Completing the follow-through, you end up with the rod tip pointed just above the target area.

The timing is considerably more complex since you have to take into consideration how far you want to cast, the direction of currents in the water, where the waves curl over to break and how fast the ensuing breaker rolls toward the shoreline. If you fail to dovetail all these points in your cast, the baited hook quite likely will come to final rest in a spot other than where you wanted to fish.

Currents, breaking waves and the rolling surf can cause the baited hook to come to rest many yards away from the intended target, which should be in one of the off-beach troughs and close to a cut knifing across a bar.

The point of aim should be the top of the sand bar just seaward of the trough in which you want to fish. Time the cast so that the terminal rig strikes the water on the back side of the curling wave. This is a relatively undisturbed patch of water in which the terminal rig will sink straight to the bottom.

Then, before the next wave reaches the spot and begins to curl and break, take enough turns on the reel handle to drag the terminal rig off the sand bar and into the trough. If you use the proper sinker shape and weight for the water turbulence encountered on the day you fish, the terminal rig will remain in the trough. So why not make the cast directly to the spot in which you want the baited hook to rest?

The most turbulence in the trough occurs when the wave curls and breaks into it. The least turbulence exists after the breaker passes on its roll toward the shoreline. How well the sinker digs into the bottom hinges on the lag time between breakers.

The longer the lag, the better the sinker purchases into the sand. A properly timed cast is the best way to prevent a crashing surf from rolling your terminal rig right back to your feet.

Take into consideration the currents running parallel to the beach. Make your cast a little upcurrent, so that when it deflects downward with the current it will come to rest where you desire to fish.

The wind, too, must be considered. A wind blowing from behind you will allow easy distance casting, but it will shorten your cast if it is blowing directly in from the open sea. Crosswinds, too, will require some compensation. In respect to the wind remember that the heavier the line, the more it will belly in crosswinds as well as in currents. You may want to use a lighter test line but compensate by putting more line on the reel.

AWAITING THE STRIKE

Big redfish have a unique way of working a bait. Most often they will nose the bait, pick it up with their lips and mouth it as they slowly swim off. If there is an undue strain on the bait, they will likely drop it and swim off. Therefore, a special touch is needed. Few surf fishermen stand at the water's edge and hold their rod while waiting for a redfish to pick up the bait. Most set their rods in surf sand spikes. This is a metal or fiberglass device pushed into the sand and into which the rod is placed.

The rod leans at about a 45-to 60-degree angle to the water. The reel is put in freespool, with the clicker button engaged and the drag set very light. After that, the surf fisherman plunks his frame into some sort of beach chair and awaits results.

There may be a wait of only a few minutes ... or an hour ... or several hours. There are some days when you quit fishing and still have the same bait you started with. In short, the waits for and between redfish pickups are often long. If you stand up, or even sit down and hold the rod all that time you'll end up with aches and pains in places you didn't know existed.

HOW REDFISH STRIKE

There are times when a bull redfish will grab the bait and take off with authority. More often, the strike will be more of a pickup. You realize a fish is carrying off the bait when the line begins to

Oversized surf redfish should be landed as quickly as possible and promptly returned to the water. Proper handling is also imperative. Support the fish with one hand beneath the head and the other below the stomach cavity. Avoid squeezing the fish, and never insert your fingers into its gills. (Photo by Larry Bozka)

pay off the reel and the clicker begins to chatter.

This is the time to lift the rod out of the sand spike, take the reel out of freespool, point the rod tip toward the fish and tighten the drag ... but only moderately. Then, sock the fish to bed the hook. The redfish has a tough mouth, so it pays to strike a couple or three times to make sure the hook penetrates. If the fish is solidly hooked, the fight after that will be a tug-of-war. Big redfish make repeated runs, but they are seldom so long in one direction as to strip all the line from a 200-yard capacity reel. The initial runs will be into the current, but as the fish tires, the runs will be more and more with the current. Never tighten the drag to the point that the fish is unable to surge and take line. An over-tightened drag could cause the hook to tear out of the fish's mouth, or it might even result in a broken line. Keep the drag sufficiently tight to maintain a steady strain on the fish.

HOW TO RELEASE REDFISH

If you are fishing the waters of a state in which it is illegal to keep big redfish, take care to release the fish as quickly as possible.

Don't fight the fish longer than necessary. Those half-hour to hour-long battles to tire big redfish on very light tackle serve no purpose other than to exhaust the fish to a point beyond recovery. I've seen too many battle-worn fish released only to struggle off, die of toxic shock and then drift up on the beach a day later.

Work the fish into knee-deep water and unhook it as gently as possible. If the hook is buried too deep in the fish's mouth, simply cut it off. The hook will rust and fall out in a matter of a few days.

If the fish is brought up from deep water, use an ice pick or similar slender sharp object to puncture the fish's swim bladder. Do this just before the fish is returned to the water. Properly executed, the procedure is harmless. The slight puncture will permit the fish to regain its balance and return to deep water. Failure to puncture the bladder may prevent the fish from diving deep, and a fish that is unable to dive deep will flounder and die at the surface of the water.

If it's an absolute must that you have a photo of yourself with the soon-to-be-released fish, get the photo-taking completed quickly. A fish out of the water more than a few minutes will die. Some marine experts say the absolute maximum out-of-the-water allowance is five minutes. Personally, I feel it is less than that in the case of big fish brought up from deep water.

Get your buddy to snap the photo of you holding the fish in ankle-deep water. Get down on your knees and keep the fish in the water while the photo is being taken. If you can't get down into the water, then hold the fish in both hands and on a horizontal plane. Support the fish with one hand *under* where the head joins the body and the other *under* the stomach and cavity.

Do not squeeze the fish. Tight squeezing can result in serious and permanent injury to the fish. Strictly taboo are grabbing the fish across the back of the head or inserting fingers in the gills.

Hang the fish up by the lips and you can congratulate yourself on having just condemned the fish to death. The weight of the fish's innards will make the organs sag and cause fatal internal injuries. Gravity is lessened greatly by the cushioning support of water when the fish is in its environment, but above the surface it's a quick killer.

We just don't have enough fish to waste for purposes of satisfying man's vanity. **BB**

7.
PIER, JETTY REDFISHING

The T-head area of a beachfront fishing pier affords the fisherman the opportunity to reach beyond the third sand bar, where schools of redfish often cruise during the fall and spring. The distance advantage becomes especially obvious when the tide is exceptionally low. (Photo by Larry Bozka)

Some people say the beachfront pier is the poor man's avenue to big game fishing. Pier concessionaires agree with the tag, but they prefer to change "poor man" to "working man." It has a better ring.

There is no question that the beachfront pier extends the reach of the shore-bound fisherman to a few of the sea's big gamefish. The bull redfish happens to be one of them. The bull redfish's less regal cousin, the bull black drum, is another.

Pier fishing for big redfish is actually an extension of surf fishing, in light of the fact that the identical same waters are fished. The pier, however, affords the fisherman the opportunity to reach beyond the third sand bar, where schools of large redfish often cruise in the fall and spring.

There are, in fact, times when the beachfront pier T-head offers the fisherman his only crack at large redfish. Those times are when extremely low tides force the redfish to remain outside of the third seaward bar.

The beachfront pier is a boon to the fisherman who seeks his redfish at night, a period when these fish are often the most active. The pier also offers the fisherman the opportunity to fish when the water is too cold or too rough for surf fishing. This cold water/rough water combination is ideal for redfish action in the fall. The chilly, rolling surf and water that is off-colored seems to entice redfish to work into shoal areas. Consequently, this works to the advantage of people fishing from piers.

PIER FISHING BASICS

If one is to be successful fishing from a beachfront pier T-head, he must tailor his gear and techniques accordingly.

First off, there is the tackle. The light tackle used in seeking reds in the bays is not suitable for pier fishing. Instead, a reasonably stout rod is necessary. It need not be as long as the true surf rod, but it must have adequate backbone.

A long rod will serve the pier fisherman in two ways. The length, of course, will enable him to make long casts, although the casts need not be as long as those required in true surf fishing from the beach or from knee-deep water. Rod length is also essential to fighting big fish hooked from the pier. The length is needed to turn a fish away and out from the pilings when it is brought in close to the pier.

If you have no gaff or landing net to get the fish onto the pier decking, a long rod is a valuable asset. The fish can be kept out of the pilings as you walk along the pier back to the beach. You can then get down on the sand and work the fish into very shallow water.

A reel capable of holding 200 to 250 yards of 30-pound test line is necessary. The fish's first run will be the longest, but it won't be nearly as long as most fishermen claim. I keep hearing tales of fish ''ripping off a hundred yards of line.'' Admittedly, it might seem like that much when you're holding the rod and watching monofilament line melt off the reel.

Actually, the first run will be more like 40 to 50 yards, after which the fish angles sideways to the pull of the line. A big redfish is not a long-distance runner. It works back and forth, and between those direction changes a good fisherman can almost always regain a considerable amount of line.

People who fish from the pier T-head will find that they need less sinker weight for holding the bait in place than when surf fishing. Except in the roughest of weather, most pier fishing will be beyond the breaking surf.

When currents are reasonably light, the fish-finder terminal rig is ideal for redfishing from a pier. It offers a big advantage in that it allows the baited hook to wave about in the current. The action helps to attract fish, and the lack of tension as the line slips through the sinker will permit the fish to better mouth the bait.

This is important if you want to get the bait deep enough in the fish's mouth for the hook to purchase. Big redfish that feel an undue amount of resistance while mouthing the bait are prone to drop it and move on to easier pickings.

The same basics that are effective in surf fishing will do equally well for the fisherman seeking his game from a pier T-head.

JETTY FISHING BASICS

Almost all redfishing from and around jetties is in deep water, mainly along the edges of channels or in holes or where there are depressions on the bottom. Most of the redfish taken via surf fishing or from beachfront piers are bulls. There is a wider range in redfish sizes in the case of jetty fishing.

Remember, almost all jetties border channels or cuts that connect the open sea with bays. These are the avenues that redfish use when they grow sufficiently large to leave the bays, and this migration to a new home in offshore waters generally starts when the fish are 25 to 30 inches long.

Age-wise, this is between three-and-one-half to four years. Accordingly, redfish caught from jetty waters can be in a range from five or six pounds to more than 40. The biggest ones will be caught in the fall.

There are two ways to fish the jetties. The "poor man" or "working man" way is to walk out on the rocks. This dictates that fishermen be as sure-footed as mountain goats in order to hop from rock to rock as they work their way out to where a channel or hole is within easy casting range.

Jetty rock-hoppers need stout, seven-to nine-foot rods. When you fish from atop the rocks, you don't play a fish a lot. The only sure way to land a big fish from atop the granite is to do it quickly. That means manhandling the fish and horsing it in. Any big redfish given its head will swim back and forth, and if it passes the line over an underwater rock, the barnacles will cut the line as quickly as the proverbial hot knife slices butter. You need a rod with backbone so you can turn the fish away from trouble areas.

Jetty rock-hoppers should use stout, seven-to nine-foot rods for two basic reasons. The backbone of the blank enables to the fisherman to land the fish quickly, and the length makes it much easier to prevent the fish from cutting the line on barnacle-encrusted rocks as it's being landed. (Photo by Joe Richard)

Like the larger jetty systems bordering navigational channels, beachfront rock groins have washed-out holes at their bases in which redfish and other species occasionally congregate. Remember, though, to be especially careful when walking the rocks. Footing can be treacherous, particularly atop rocks that are covered with algae and moss. (Photo by Larry Bozka)

The easiest and most comfortable way to fish jetty waters for redfish is from a boat. You can anchor the boat along the edge of the stepoff of a channel or right over a hole. As a result, much of the fishing may be almost straight down.

This situation eliminates the need to use big sinkers that dig into the bottom. All you need is sufficient weight to overcome the current and get the bait to the bottom.

Most jetty boaters use double-drop terminal rigs because this rig saves time that would otherwise be spent retrieving and re-baiting the hook. The two-hook stagings on a double-drop terminal rig eliminate some of this work.

A popular second choice for jetty fishing is, again, the versatile fish-finder terminal rig. The fish-finder is excellent to use provided there is sufficient current to swing the bait around.

Years ago, jetty rocks were often splotched with various colors of paint. This was in the days before depth sounders. Fishermen used to break jars of leftover paint on the rocks to mark the location of favorite fishing holes.

Depth sounders have dramatically changed that, and today it is not uncommon to see boaters watching their LED screens for holes and signs of fish in holes as they slowly cruise along the edge of the rocks.

Considerable numbers of redfish congregate in the holes along jetties when there are substantial currents. The fish fan out over much wider areas when currents are light.

It is not uncommon when jetty fishing to find redfish in the same holes day after day. If you locate the boat precisely over a hole you catch fish, but miss the hole by a few dozen yards and you

This magnificent bull red, caught near the South Galveston jetty, was kept alive in a special holding tank and transported to the John Wilson Redfish Hatchery in Flour Bluff, Texas. Deep holes near jetty rocks provide the fish refuge from the current, and are therefore most productive when the tide is running strong. (Photo by Joe Richard)

may not lose a bait.

The best periods for redfishing at the jetties are in the fall and spring. Bull redfish are most often found in the fall, with most of them working along the beach sides of the jetties. Bull redfish are caught in lesser numbers during the spring. Most of the reds caught in the spring range from about seven to 12 pounds, and most of them are taken from holes on the channel side of the rocks or along the slopes of the channels.

The slowest redfish action in jetty water occurs in the winter. There are, however, exceptions to the rule. During unusually mild winters, the major spawn run of big redfish almost overlaps the minor spawning run of spring.

Redfish, mostly fish weighing up to about 12 pounds, sometimes abound in holes along jetties when winter temperatures are unusually frigid. Major temperature drops and freezes cause the fish to move from shallow bays to waters that are warmer. That warmer water is in the holes along the jetties. **BB**

8.
WEATHER
AND REDFISH

Sustained freezing temperatures send redfish scurrying for deep water ... not only open-water holes and depressions, but also rivers and deep canals that empty into bays. Matagorda, Texas fishing guide Ron Frasier used a soft plastic lead-headed jig to dupe this Colorado River red. (Photo by Larry Bozka)

The redfish is found year-round throughout the Gulf Coast states. Small redfish in the bays are likely to be taken at virtually any time, although they may temporarily leave a bay if the food supply becomes seriously depleted. Big redfish are usually year-round fish in the deep holes adjacent to jetties or around the mouths of passes and cuts. Although big reds can be found throughout the year in the surf, they are most plentiful in beachfront waters during the spring and fall spawning seasons.

Weather along the Gulf Coast states exerts a considerable influence over redfish, particularly the large ones. During the heat of summer the big fish often roam close to shore, but not necessarily in the surf. Instead, the bulls will move about in the deep channels and holes that may be within a few miles of the beach. Likely places to seek these fish include the depressions and craters in the vicinity of jetties and around offshore oil rigs.

A depth sounder is an invaluable aid for this kind of fishing. The holes may be of considerable depth in comparison to the general level of the surrounding bottom, or not much more than shallow depressions a few feet deeper than the adjacent area. The deepest holes are generally around the ends of jetties, where strong currents flow.

The weather always plays a major role in regard to which holes the fish may frequent. In fair weather and with only light currents and a basically flat sea, fishermen should look for the reds to be in depressions. If there are a number of depressions in the immediate area, look for the fish to be moving back and forth between these submerged craters.

You won't need a lot of sinker weight for this fishing, and you can expect the best results if you use a fish-finder terminal rig. Since the water is usually fairly clear on a calm, light-current day, a good choice of baits is large live shrimp or live mullet. The action of the bait will help to attract the attention of fish.

Fish the deep holes in rough weather, especially if strong currents prevail. A prime area to fish when the water is rough is alongside jetties. Fish the calmest side of the jetty, which will be on the side away from the direction of the wind.

Waves breaking on the rocks and currents churning through the boulders wash out marine fodder that stimulates redfish into feeding. The fish will be on the calm side, quite close to the rocks. There, they wait to pick off marine life washed out of the rocks.

Following a period of heavy rainfall, reduced salinity levels push speckled trout out of the bays in search of saltier surroundings. However, redfish are virtually unaffected by the change, and will stay behind to feed upon small baitfish driven to the bottom by the freshwater surface layer. (Photo by Joe Richard)

I have caught a lot of big redfish on days when the water was so rough that in order to maintain my balance I had to keep one arm around a stanchion or looped through a rail on the boat. Fishing in rough weather is neither easy nor is it particularly pleasant, but it certainly is a time when big redfish are apt to roam.

Some of the most rewarding surf fishing for large reds I have ever enjoyed took place in a very heavy surf. I have fished the surf on days when strong offshore winds caused large waves to show whitecaps almost all the way to the horizon. Those were days when the waves began to curl over and break a good quarter of a mile offshore. From there they came rolling shoreward, a boiling, cascading succession of white water racing to the sandy beach. The force of each breaker would push water many feet up the slope of the beach before the wave lost its momentum and drained back to the Gulf of Mexico.

Under conditions like that it is not uncommon to use a six- to eight-ounce specially designed surf sinker to hold the baited hook where the fish roam. It is difficult to cast into the wind, and you never get the distance you desire. Even if you wade out knee-deep before casting, you still get soaking wet because of breaking waves that forcefully dash against your legs.

Naturally, beachfront tides are pushed quite high when the wind barrels in from straight offshore. That, along with the fact that the powerful surf makes the water very sandy, may be the combination that lures big redfish closer to the beach than usual. Whatever the reason, the big fish enter water that at most is about waist-deep ... not a lot of water for a 25-to 30-pound bull red.

There is no question about the rough water churning marine life free from the bottom. The dying breakers that race up the slope of the beach deposit all kinds of live mollusks on the sand.

I really believe rough water may offer the most exciting of all surf fishing for redfish. Big redfish put up a strong fight in the calmest of water conditions, but when aided by a crashing surf and a strong current they are supreme tackle-testers.

I find something contagious about a wild surf. To me, it's stimulating and exciting. My wife says I must be out of my mind to do it, but I find it adventurous to stand on the Galveston Seawall and watch the storm-generated waves charge in from the Gulf.

The power of white water, whether it is storm-driven or tumbling down a canyon of rapids, is awesome.

IN THE BAYS

One of the good things about fishing for redfish in bays is that, unlike speckled trout, redfish don't require calm and clear water. Forget speckled trout when the bay is rough and sandy. The same water conditions, however, can pay solid dividends when one is seeking redfish.

Based on personal experience, this is one of the few times when I consider still fishing to be the most productive way to work a bay. Rough, sandy water is going to knock out hopes of locating fish by sight. You won't be able to see slicks or tailing fish, and there won't be any bait scurrying around on the surface. Bait and small fish go to the bottom in rough weather, where they will be less vulnerable to the chop and waves.

Louisiana fishing guide Terry Shaughnessy took this six-pound redfish from the mouth of a bayou that empties into Lake Calcasieu. Rainfall and its subsequent runoff carry nutrients out of the marshes and into the bayous, and eventually the saltgrass fringes of adjacent bays. Those nutrients attract forage species which in turn are preyed upon by hungry redfish. (Photo by Larry Bozka)

Rough, sandy conditions can plague a bay for lengthy periods. I have seen times when a bay was rough and sandy for a week straight. I will not consider fishing for specks when a bay is like that.

Nevertheless, if you know bay structure ... preferably grass stands, points and live reefs ... a dirty bay is worth working for reds. Small fish normally congregate in such areas, and will still be there in rough weather. They will concentrate in whatever nearby shelter exists.

Just because the water may be dirty for a week doesn't mean the redfish stop feeding for a week. They get just as hungry in dirty water as in clear water, but have to exert more effort to find the matter upon which they feed.

And the easiest way to find food in sandy water is, pardon the pun, a smelly business. It's all done by scent, and redfish have highly developed scent receptors. Thus, the sandy water situation is ideal for the still fisherman who uses natural bait and has the patience for this kind of fishing. You need to be aware that at its best this kind of fishing is nonetheless slow.

RAIN, FRESHWATER RUNOFF

In regard to some species of fish, the most notable being speckled trout, rain and freshwater runoff can stop the action as fast as the lights go out when you hit the wall switch. Happily, the redfish is not among them. In fact, the redfish is a species that often becomes quite active when rain pelts the surface.

A light rain or drizzle won't bother speckled trout. In areas where the water surface is quite calm, a light rain can stimulate schoolie-size trout into feeding. Not so with a heavy downpour. The heavy rain will dilute saltwater to the point that trout simply move to other areas which offer salinity levels more to their liking. The same thing happens with freshwater runoff from the flooding of a bay's watershed.

Redfish are not affected the same way. They readily remain in areas where the water is quite fresh, as long as there is sufficient marine life upon which they can forage. The rain and runoff will cause small baitfish to go to the bottom, where the water is saltiest. That's great, since redfish are bottom-feeders anyway.

Some of my most exciting bay redfish catches were made along the edges of marshes on very rainy days. You can see the color of the water change as mud-clouded runoff drains first off the land into the marshes and next into the bay proper. Use natural baits and fish the border of the sandy water fringing a marsh. There, the dividends can be rich. Forget about artificial lures, because the water will be much too sandy.

One of the most overlooked fishing spots along the Gulf Coast is the Intracoastal Waterway, which stretches from northern Florida to the southern tip of Texas. This waterway can be very productive of redfish during the fall and spring if there is heavy rainfall on the bordering land masses, many of which are saltgrass marshes. The freshwater runoff naturally flows into the waterway itself, carrying with it all sorts of nutrients that attract small

When water conditions are sandy and natural baits are scarce, a gold or silver spoon is often a productive alternative. The wobbling metal lures are highly reflective and will appeal to a gamefish's sense of sight when other lures cannot. (Photo by Joe Richard)

baitfish. The small fish in turn stimulate redfish to feed. There, again, are the ever-present rungs of Mother Nature's food ladder.

FOUL WEATHER BAIT

There is only one kind of bait to use for redfish in foul weather conditions: fresh natural bait. This is one of those occasions when dead bait or cut bait is actually superior to live bait.

The darting and wiggling of live bait is fish-attracting, but only if the fish can see the bait. That isn't likely when the water is rough and sandy and you can't see more than a foot or so below the surface.

Live bait has a scent that can be detected by the redfish. That scent, however, can be magnified if the bait is cut or broken so that it oozes natural juices. Fresh dead shrimp, small fish and small blue crabs are the most effective baits for foul weather fishing.

One of the most effective aids I have found for foul weather fishing is the fish attractant. These are marketed by a number of companies, and are available in spray, liquid and solid form. Use those specially manufactured for use in saltwater.

Since you are involved in still fishing, the repeated use of a fish attractant on each bait will cause a very effective scent chum line. Fish crossing the chum line often detour to follow the line to its point of origin.

Still fishing may start off slow and remain that way for an hour or two, but if you establish a scent or chum line, you can usually enjoy some surprisingly good action before the trip is over. Bear in mind, though, that rough water tends to break up and dissipate a chum line. In order for the line to be effective, the attractant should be liberally applied to every bait used. **BB**

9.
SPECIAL GEAR

Surf fishing is often done with several rods, and the wait between bites can be long and tiresome. Rod holders, known by surf casters as "sand spikes," are therefore essential gear. A three-to four-foot section of PVC pipe makes a dandy sand spike. (Photo by Joe Richard)

If your game plan is redfishing on a grand scale, you will need some special gear other than rod, reel, line and suitable terminal tackle.

By chance, a fisherman can land a fish without means geared to the fish. Fishing, however, is at best a chancy sport. And "by chance" is not an efficient way to fish.

You can't catch a fish unless you take the chance of getting a bait or lure into the water. If you fish strictly "by chance," you will never be sure of what you might catch. In this book the target is the redfish. So minimize the chance element by going prepared.

The largest redfish I almost caught was just that, an "almost caught" red, because I went fishing unprepared. That occurred in August of 1938. I recall the month and year because it was just a week or 10 days before I enrolled as a freshman in the University of Texas at Austin. I wanted to get in a final fishing trip before I went to school.

The trip was to the surf, about 15 miles down West Galveston Island. I had been fishing for about an hour, losing a couple of baits and having one brief hookup in the period. Then I had a pickup that took line off the reel at a steady clip.

I reacted properly in permitting the fish to run with the bait for a few seconds before striking. I struck, and the hookup seemed solid enough. The fish just kept swimming along at a steady pace, and line continued to peel off the reel. Only this time, it was under the protest of the drag.

I struck a second time to better set the hook. It was then that the fish felt the bite of the hook. The fish surged straight out and then turned and swam parallel to the beach. I started walking down the beach with it, tightening the drag and trying to regain line little by little.

As I recall, the fish was in about four feet of water. Redfish don't jump, but this one came to the surface and rolled. That's when I saw the size of the fish. It had to be four feet long. Its massive tail flashed out of the water, and the black spot looked as big as a silver dollar.

I managed to pick up some line by continuing to walk along parallel to the fish's run, only this time I waded out about knee-deep in the surf. I don't know how long I battled the fish in this manner. It seemed like an eternity, although I suspect it was probably no more than about 15 minutes.

I reacted as most inexperienced fishermen do. The size of the fish prompted me to think "get it in quick before it gets away." So I tightened the drag and started horsing the fish, and I got it into knee-deep water.

The problem was that it was still a green fish, one full of energy and fight. I had a gaff, but I had left it at the car, more than a hundred yards down the beach. So, I tried to grab the fish with my hands, and that was all the fish needed to spur it into a new, and successful, surge for freedom.

The rod was snatched momentarily from under my arm. I grabbed it in time, but the line looped over the rod tip.

"*Pop!*" went the line and there went my trophy redfish, triumphantly finning its way out into the Gulf of Mexico.

I would like to believe it would have been a state record. Down through the years, and quite often in recent years, I have thought of that fish. I would have landed it if I had: (1) carried the

The castnet is an important tool for the serious redfish angler, but the device is only as effective as its upkeep. This castnet illustrates what can happen after repeated casting. The draw lines twist when the net spins on each cast, and twisted draw lines impede proper opening and closing of the net. The twist can be removed through lifting the net by the metal ring and allowing it to slowly revolve. (Photo by A.C. Becker, Jr.)

gaff with me, (2) made proper use of the reel's drag and loosened it instead of trying to grab the fish, (3) fought the fish longer instead of trying to horse it in, and (4) overcome the buck fever I suffered when I first saw the size of the creature.

All I can do is sum up the event by the numbers: (1) dumb, (2) dumb, (3) dumb) and (4) dumb.

LANDING DEVICES

In light of today's restrictive bag and slot length limits, it is important to use landing devices that are not harmful to the fish.

The gaff, the tried-and-true device for landing big fish, is a suitable choice only in those areas where it is legal to retain big redfish. A gaff is an effective landing device because the tool's point is spiked deep into the flesh. A gaff wound in the lower part of the fish will cause internal injuries which are almost always fatal. Gaff wounds in the head or gills are definitely fatal. The least injury to the fish will be inflicted if the gaff can be bedded in the body just a few inches from the base of the tail. But that takes skillful use of the device. Thus, a gaff is the wrong instrument to use if the fish is to be released.

If you fish areas in which it is legal to retain bull redfish and you choose to do so, use a gaff when fishing the surf, and either a long-handled gaff or a flying gaff when fishing from a pier or a boat. Most pay fishing piers have long-handled gaffs available for their customers.

A gaff, however, is only as effective as the sharpness of its point. A dull point is difficult to drive into the fish's flesh, and if it strikes and glances off without penetrating, it may be just the spur to put a burst of energy in the fish. Often, an unexpected surge will win the fish its freedom.

Then there's the flying gaff. This can be a dangerous weapon that can backfire and injure the fisherman. A flying gaff is one that is released from the handle after it is driven into the fish. The gaff hook is attached to the end of a rope which the fisherman uses to pull in the fish.

As long as the handle is in the gaff and someone is holding the handle, there is considerable control over the fish. After the gaff hook is released from the handle, though, it's an entirely different situation.

The person holding the rope can control the fish only one way, and that is to pull. The fish, however, can whip back and forth. If the gaff hook is only lightly bedded, the metal device can be ripped from the flesh and propelled toward the person pulling on the rope.

LANDING NETS

Landing nets come in many sizes and several styles. A net with a three-to four-foot-long handle is suitable when one is fishing

These commercially-manufactured surf spikes have triangular flanges which, when shoved completely into the sand, will prevent the device from tipping over under pressure. Crossover latches assure the rod will not fall out. PVC plastic versions are also commercially available, and because they will not rust, are preferred by some fishermen. (Photo by A.C. Becker, Jr.)

from a small boat. A similar net with a two-to three-foot handle is more manageable for wade fishing.

The ideal net is one that floats. If the handle is light metal or PVC pipe, you can make the net a floater by filling it with foam peanuts and capping the ends.

Special landing nets are needed for pier fishing because piers are so high above the water. I've seen some pier nets with extra-long 15-to 20-foot handles. Under the best of conditions, these are difficult to use. Extra-long-handled nets of this sort are most likely to be found on pay fishing piers.

The most practical landing nets for pier use are drop-nets. The net bag is attached to a three-to four-foot diameter metal ring, which in turn is attached to a long rope with a bridle. The net is dropped into the water and held so it is several feet below the surface.

Proper use of the device dictates leading the fish over the net and then quickly hauling it up. Start pulling up immediately after the head of the fish is a little over halfway across the net. When the fish feels the rim of the net hit its body it will dive, and that dive will carry it right into the bag of the net. If you start pulling up when the fish's head is beyond or over the net's rim, the creature's efforts to survive will cause it to slide over and out of the net.

FISH-GRIPPERS

There are devices on the market called fish-grippers, and most operate like vise-grip pliers. Squeeze the handle on these and the jaws close tight. Some, on the other hand, release when you release your grip on the handle. Others require releasing a latch.

Fish-grippers are excellent for wade fishing and for handling redfish in the surf. Reds to be retained can be gripped across the top and just behind the head. If the fish is to be released, then grab it near the base of the tail.

The only problem with fish-grippers is that they have metal parts, and whenever saltwater is involved, you can expect metal to rapidly rust or corrode.

The grippers should be attached to a line that in turn is tied to your belt. Some boaters who use them attach a line and a large float so the device can be recovered if dropped overboard.

BAIT CONTAINERS

A bait container is an absolute must if you plan to use any kind

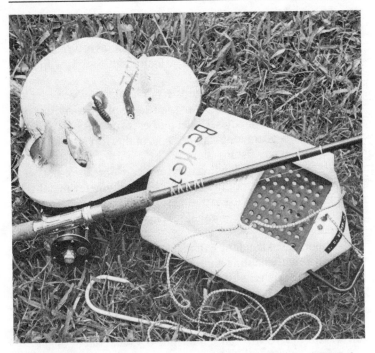

The rounded corners of most bait containers prevent baitfish and shrimp from injuring themselves. A bait container is only as good as the water it contains. (Photo by A.C. Becker, Jr.)

of live bait.

Those made of wood or plastic are the most durable in saltwater. Metal live bait containers are fine if they are galvanized so as to resist the ravages of saltwater.

Regardless of the material used in the construction of bait containers, don't paint them. Most paints have toxic ingredients that can be fatal to the bait if the paint flakes off and suspends within the container.

Use a container that will float, and when wade fishing tow it behind on a length of cord. Bait containers can be used when fishing from piers, but you will need a rope long enough to lower the container to the water. Bait containers contain water, but unless that water can circulate and dilute with the sea or bay water, it will quickly foul and cause bait to die.

If the bait is to be transported any distance, lower the water temperature by adding a few small chunks of ice to slow the metabolism of the bait. When you reach the fishing area, slowly bring the water temperature within the container to that of the water in which you will be fishing. A very sudden temperature change from warm to cold or vice-versa can kill bait.

Use a container that's round or oval in shape. Containers with corners can cause bait loss if the bait butts hard against the walls. Bait in an oval or round container will tend to swim around and around in the same direction. The bait may scrape against the side, but it won't butt abruptly.

CASTNETS, MINNOW TRAPS

Bait camps may not always stock the kind of live bait you prefer to use for redfish. Thus, the serious redfish angler ought to have some equipment for catching his own.

Start with the castnet. This is an ideal device for the capture of all sorts of bait, including grass shrimp, mullet, mud minnows, pinfish and small blue crabs.

Purchase a net of a size that you can throw. As an example, a net that will cover a 10-foot diameter circle of bottom is fine if you can make it fully open on every cast. If you can't handle a net that size ... and most people can't ... then go with a smaller one that you know will fully open on every cast.

There is no formula for picking the right size. You simply have to try different sizes and then go with what you can best handle. Whether you get a net made of linen, cotton, nylon or monofilament line depends upon what you want to spend and how much care you give it. Wash a net in fresh water and then dry it after every trip, and that net will last for many years. Abuse the net and you can plan on buying a replacement every few years.

Live mullet, mud minnows and small pinfish make excellent redfish baits. Problem is, relatively few bait establishments stock them because they are much less in demand than are live shrimp. The solution is to go catch your own with a minnow trap.

Bait the trap with chunks of stale bread and set it in water deep enough to completely cover it. Place the trap along the fringe of a saltgrass marsh or the edge of a slough or bayou. Put the trap out late on the afternoon prior to the day you plan to fish.

SAND SPIKES

A sand spike is an absolute must if you surf fish for redfish. The waits between bites can be long and tiresome, and if you stand there holding the rod and reel the entire time you will become a very weary person before the day ends.

A sand spike is simply a device that is shoved into the bottom a few feet out from the beach. Sink it into the sand at an angle of about 45 to 60 degrees toward the water.

A landing net with a three-to four-foot-long handle is well suited adequate when fishing from a small boat. The ideal net is one that floats. Some, with handles constructed with light metal or PVC pipe, can be filled with foam peanuts to make them buoyant. (Photo by A.C. Becker, Jr.)

Most sand spikes have a triangular flange about six to eight inches above the tip that is shoved into the bottom. This flange, when shoved completely into the sand, will prevent the spike from tipping over. The butt of the fishing rod is placed in a short, can-like container about 18 to 24 inches from the top of the spike. There are usually several crossover latches to hold the rod in place. The crossovers should have quick-releases so you can get the rod out in a hurry.

Always shove the spike into the bottom where there is a few inches of water. This will help it to pack tight and stand. A sand spike will not hold if you try to sink it in dry sand.

A fisherman can make his own sand spikes out of three-to four-foot lengths of PVC pipe that can be purchased at a hardware store. Three-inch diameter pipe will suffice unless your rod has a large cork or rubber butt-end. Then you will have to buy pipe of a diameter that will accommodate the butt-end. A lot of surf anglers like the cork or rubber balls because they make for more comfortable fishing when fighting a large fish.

Sharpen a point on the end of the pipe that is to be shoved into the sand. The pipe will bed firmly, because the inside of the part shoved into the sand will fill and pack with sand. Again, make sure it is shoved into the bottom where there is water so that the sand will pack tight.

To use the home-made sand spike simply stick the rod butt into the open end at the top. The rod will go down in the pipe until the rim comes in contact with the reel. To use the rod to set the hook and battle the fish, simply pull the butt out of the pipe.

In areas where vehicles can be driven right up to the edge of the water, some surf fishermen attach lengths of PVC pipe to the car or truck's bumper. But a word of warning when parking a vehicle near the water's edge: Watch the rising tide. The vehicle's tires will sink quite fast and firm in the sand when the water swirls around them. **BB**

10.
REEL CONTROL

It's safe to assume that more fishermen lose fish because of an improperly set reel drag than for any other reason. Redfish make powerful surges upon seeing the boat or landing net, and the inexperienced angler often reacts by tightening the drag. If the fish doesn't break the line, it's just as likely to tear free of the hook. (Photo by Larry Bozka)

n the preceding chapter I related my experience with the biggest redfish I "almost caught," a fish I still like to believe would have been a Texas state record. I lost the fish because I didn't understand how to properly use the star drag on my reel.

Down through the years of my fishing experiences and writing about the sport I have seen a great many cases of drag misuse. I have seen it occur with all types and sizes of reels. The errors in misuse have resulted in lost fish, broken rods, and even rods and reels being snatched out of the user's hands.

The free-spool lever, which when engaged prevents the reel spindle from revolving, and the drag are two of the most functional gadgets on the modern fishing reel.

The free-spool lever is the easiest of the two to understand and use. You put the reel in free-spool when you want to cast, which permits the spindle to spin freely. Engaged with the free-spool lever, the spindle revolves only when the handle is turned or when the pull on the line overcomes the friction of the drag.

The purpose of the drag is widely understood, but its purpose is abused and misused. Some people screw the drag down as tight as possible, and some tighten it moderately and then never touch it again. Then there are those who frequently tighten or loosen the drag during the process of fighting a large or stubborn fish.

So which is correct?

TIGHTENING, LOOSENING

The star drag on conventional wind and many spincast reels can be adjusted while you're turning the crank handle to pick up line. This can be done all at the same time and with one hand.

Though some spinning reels feature rear-mounted drags, most of the larger models used for redfishing do not. Either way, the person using the reel usually has to let go of the reel handle in order to adjust the drag dial on the reel's face. You can do it with one hand when fishing with a small spinning reel, but it becomes a bit of a chore with a large reel ... particularly the size used for surf casting and pier fishing.

The correct use of the drag is tightening and/or loosening during the course of your scrap with the fish. In the case of bay fishing, you may set the drag when you start the day and never change it during the remainder of the trip. On the other hand, if you're fishing waters which hold a wide range of species you may

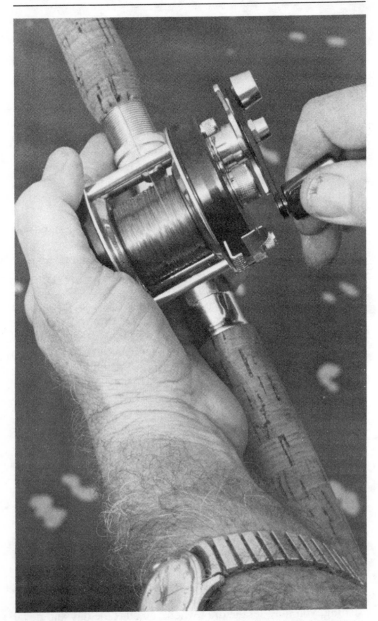

Note how this fisherman is "palming" the reel. The rod handle extends under the forearm, which acts as a brace when the hook is set. (Photo by A.C. Becker, Jr.)

have to make frequent drag changes.

The primary purpose of the drag is to maintain tension on the fish. That constant strain is what whips the fish. The drag should be set tight enough to maintain steady pressure on the fish, yet loose enough for the line to be stripped off the reel in the event the fish makes a sudden or very strong run. You run the risk of a broken line, broken rod tip or both if you tighten the drag to the fullest.

That raises another question: How tight is tight enough? A few reels have dials that indicate in poundage how much pull is required to strip off line. If you want a reel like that, be prepared to spend a good chunk of money. A true big game fisherman needs that kind of reel, but that kind of reel isn't necessary for big redfish ... even if you do fish a couple of times a week.

You can properly adjust the drag tension by simply testing the pull. After you set the drag, grab the line a foot or so from the reel and pull. If you have to jerk to get the drag started and allow the spindle to turn, the drag is set much too tight. You want the spindle to turn when a steady, reasonably strong pull is applied, and you want it to turn smoothly. A drag that chatters or causes the spindle to revolve in erratic jerks is one that's ready to give you serious problems.

Additional adjustments on the drag are always necessary when you're fighting a fish, with the general rule being "the larger the fish, the more frequent the adjustments."

REEL PHYSICS

When a fish is hooked, it is only human to try to prevent the fish from taking line off the reel. Thus, it is human nature to tighten the drag as line melts off the spindle.

Putting it mildly, this is an incorrect move ... one that can lead to tearing the hook from the fish's mouth, a broken line or broken rod tip. Always keep in mind that the fisherman who is willing to surrender line to a surging fish by loosening the drag occasionally stands the best chance of defeating the fish. It's a game of give-and-take.

Physics comes into play at this point. The strain required to strip line off the reel increases as the radius of the reel spindle and the line it carries decreases. The equation is a simple one.

To determine the strain necessary to strip off line against the original pre-strike drag setting, divide the original radius of the spindle and line at the time of the cast by the new radius of the

Fly fishing exemplifies the point that a fishing reel is intended to store line, not "reel in" a fish. It's the rod, not the reel, which applies the necessary pressure to tire the fish. (Photo by Joe Richard)

spindle and line. This is usually at the end of the fish's first run, a time when the fish is getting its "second wind" to run again.

The formula?

$$\text{Original drag setting} \times \frac{\text{Original radius}}{\text{New radius}} = \text{new drag setting}$$

(Original Drag Setting multiplied by Original Radius and divided by New Radius equals New Drag Setting)

This is easiest to understand if we use some actual figures in the equation. Consider the spindle/line radius of the typical conventional wind surf fishing reel.

The spindle/line radius is 3 inches at the time of the cast. It is reduced to 2 inches after the cast and when the fish ends its first run. The strain required to strip off line before the cast is 10 pounds.

The pounds (10) times the original radius (3) divided by the new radius (2) equals 15. That (15 pounds) is how much strain is necessary to overcome the drag and pull line off the reel.

Suppose that prior to the cast you tighten the drag to the extent that it requires 25 pounds of pull to strip off line. Using the same equation and an identical reel, but substituting 25 for the 10, the new strain required to take off line following the end of the cast and the fish's first run would be 37.5 pounds. That could mean trouble if you're using 30-pound-test line.

Furthermore, if you use the wrong kind of knot the line strength can be reduced by as much as 50 percent. In that case, you're in deep trouble.

The proper method is to ease off the drag tension as line is stripped from the reel. You may or may not have to renew tension as you recover line. This will depend on how much and how fast the fish tires.

When the redfish is brought close enough to see the fisherman or the boat, the creature is practically certain to make a couple of new surges in hopes of freeing itself from the hook. Inexperienced fishermen often panic at this point and, again, excessively tighten the drag.

Pop! There goes the fish.

The correct reaction on the part of the fisherman is to not touch the drag, much less tighten it. Work the fish close by pumping with the rod. This means pulling the fish in by lifting the rod perpendicular. Then, as you drop the rod tip back toward the fish, reel to regain line. Pump and reel. Pump and reel.

When the fish seems to be thoroughly beat and ready for the gaff or landing net, there is one more drag adjustment to make. This is when you loosen it a bit, going on the assumption that the fish still has one last spark that will ignite when contact is made with the net or gaff. This last spark may be just enough to jerk the rod out of your hands.

Play it safe, and be willing to surrender a bit of line to the fish that may still be a little green. The expression ''green fish'' means the creature still has fight left in it. This is something I failed to consider when I lost that huge redfish in 1938.

DRAG CARE

A drag is only as good as the care you give it. The device will function best when it is clean, and all of the friction disks and washers within the mechanism are in good repair.

Occasionally disassemble the drag and clean all the parts. Replace any disks that show wear, but when reassembling do not oil or grease parts in the drag. Oil or grease will cause the device to slip. A drag works best when it is dry and clean.

Adjusting the drag on an open-faced spinning reel is not an easy task for the fisherman dealing with an angry redfish in a rolling surf, as it is virtually impossible without taking your hand off the reel handle. As it is integrated into the handle assembly, the star drag on conventional level reels greatly simplifies the job. (Photo by Larry Bozka)

When the reel is put into storage until the next fishing trip, back off the tension on the drag. A reel stored for a long period and with tension on the drag can suffer major damage. The pressure of the tension can press the disks out of shape and cause the drag to chatter like a machine gun.

REEL'S REAL PURPOSE

"Reel the fish in."

We hear this expression all the time when a fisherman describes his trip. We also read it just as often when an outdoor writer pens a story for an outdoors journal. Whether the expression is spoken or written, it is totally incorrect.

Many fishermen don't know the real purpose of a fishing reel, regardless of the type. It is not a device for either reeling or pulling in a fish. Pure and simple, a fishing reel is a storage device. The fishing reel is a device for the storage of line until you make a cast. It is designed and constructed to spool off line evenly and smoothly when the cast is made. Hence, it is an aid to casting. The fishing reel is a storage device for extra line when you're battling a fish, and it is a storage device for keeping line from tangling when the fish is being brought to net or gaff.

The piece of fishing equipment that brings your redfish within reach of net or gaff is the rod. You use it to turn the fish one way or the other, pumping it in order to bring the fish nearer and pick up line for storage on the reel.

Few fishermen ever really "reel in" a fish unless it's a mighty small one. **BB**

11.
WHAT LIES
AHEAD

These large redfish are residents of the John Wilson Redfish Hatchery at Flour Bluff, Texas. The world's first operational saltwater redfish hatchery, it was constructed through a cooperative effort between the Texas Parks and Wildlife Department, Central Power and Light Company and the Gulf Coast Conservation Association. The Houston-based GCCA has done much to protect the future of coastal sport fishing, and now has local chapters throughout the Gulf and Atlantic coasts. For information, call: 713/626-GCCA. (Photo by Joe Richard)

henever one notes both bag and size limits on a fish, the thought that usually flashes in one's mind is that this particular fish is in trouble, perhaps even on the verge of being endangered. This is not the case of the redfish.

Yes, the population is down. But the numbers are not down to the point of imminent danger. The purpose of the bag, possession and slot limits on the redfish is to protect what we have so as to ensure the resource for the future. These regulations are intended to protect the redfish from the threat of indiscriminate over-harvest.

Redfish are most susceptible to loss when they are young. Fish under about 15 inches in length are very easy to catch. If you get into a school of fish this size, it is not difficult to catch one on every few casts if you use artificial lures and one on literally every cast if you fish natural bait. Small redfish are not easy to spook when they are massed in big schools, and when they start to feed, they do so with a vengeance, seeming to compete with each other to get to the bait first.

Up until the mid-1960s redfish were quite plentiful in Texas bays, and there were numerous fishing trips on which I caught several dozen of these fish in the space of a couple of hours.

Redfish become more selective in their feeding and certainly more cautious as they grow older. If the big bulls fed with the same reckless abandon as the little ones, the redfish population would indeed be threatened.

The minimum length limits are intended to get the fish past that period of life when they are most susceptible to being caught. Hopefully, many will reach the other end of the cycle, the time when they are old enough to spawn. That occurs when the fish are about four years old or in excess of 28 to 30 inches in length, and is the reason why so many states currently have maximum length limits. These laws were enacted to protect the breeders.

When I caught my first redfish back in the early 1930s, the only regulation on the species was a maximum length requirement which pertained to marketing the fish. At the time, the regulation prohibited the sale of any redfish 35 inches or longer with head-on or 32 inches long with head-off.

Daily bag, possession and length limits, and in some instances slot limits, currently vary from state to state. This is confusing for people crossing back and forth between states. As it stands now,

Catching a redfish is an experience a child is not likely to forget. Responsible management of the resource combined with protection of nursery areas and other habitat will do much to preserve the redfish for the fishermen of tomorrow. (Photo by A.C. Becker, Jr.)

one Gulf Coast state has a daily bag of three and a possession limit of six for two days of fishing. Right across the border, the neighboring state has a daily limit of 25 redfish and speckled trout in the aggregate. Still another state has a closed season on redfish during the spring.

Competent biologists and game and fish management groups seriously doubt that the redfish will ever be taken off the gamefish list. Most expect more tightening of regulations in the years to come. Most want uniform regulations across the range of the fish, and a few advocate a closed season on redfish during the seasonal spawns. Such a closure would not prohibit catching redfish, because there is no way the fish can be prevented from taking a bait or lure if it is in the water. The closed season as such would instead outlaw retention of the fish.

Bag limits are structured to prevent over-harvest of these fine gamefish. Unfortunately, there are many fishermen who will not stop catching and retaining fish as long as those fish continue to bite. These are fishermen who have to be protected from themselves.

Without regulations which impose substantial penalties for over-harvest, there will always be people who catch and keep fish as if there is no tomorrow. These are the people who reason that since they only fish once or twice a month, they should therefore be allowed to keep everything they land to make up for the days on which they didn't go fishing.

INFLUENCES ON POPULATION

Over-harvest is not always the primary reason for fish populations to decrease. More serious causes for depletion are pollution and loss of habitat. Both are caused by man.

At best, the ecology of coastal and inshore waters is quite fragile. It doesn't take a whole lot to upset the balance of nature. We tend to look at the water immediately under our noses and overlook the fact that occurrences on the land or watershed hundreds of miles inland can have devastating effects on our fish populations.

There was a time, in fact just a couple of decades ago, when all sorts of insecticides and pesticides were used on the nation's cropland. They were used in broadcast style, and some of the residue remained toxic for many years after the chemicals were initially spread. Excessive rainfall and floods carried much of the lethal residue to the coast and into our bay systems.

The problem was most acute in those bay systems located on the outflow of major rivers. Fortunately, the more dangerous and long-lasting of the pesticides have been banned and are no longer being used on our croplands.

But there is another kind of pollution that could occur at any hour of any day. And regardless of when and where it occurs, the blame must be placed on man. The trigger could be human error, carelessness, mechanical failure or simply an accident.

Our economy and society is geared to chemical production: oil, gas and the like. These products have to be transported by pipelines, trucks, ships and rail cars, and every time there is a disruption in the flow the result is pollution. How serious that pollution is depends upon whether it has a short-term or long-term effect. The long-term effect invariably means loss of habitat.

This is the most serious loss that can befall our tidal and inshore waters, because this means loss of marine life breeding and rearing grounds.

Man reduces the amount of marine life rearing areas by cutting canals and creating new waterways across bays, building water-front developments, and simply draining marshes and reclaiming lands for man-made structures: industrial complexes, hotels, golf courses, airports and more.

Regulations on the fish themselves protect the overall redfish population through various stages of life. Even more important is the preservation of those vital portions of the coastal environment appropriately called "nursery areas." Invariably, these are marshes and grass flats. This dwindling form of marine habitat is especially critical in the fall, when redfish and other fish species spawn.

All of the spawning occurs in the Gulf of Mexico and the western Atlantic Ocean. The fish drop their eggs, and the eggs hatch in about 20 to 40 hours.

Assisted by the currents, the larval fish move through passes

The survival rate of inch-long fingerlings is substantially higher than that of microscopic redfish fry. How many of these fish grow old enough to reproduce, however, is a much-debated topic among marine biologists. Estimates range from a fraction of a percentage point to an optimistic 10 percent. (Photo by Larry Bozka)

and into the bays. From there, they seek the nursery areas, where they ultimately find the food and shelter so critical to their survival.

RESTORATION EFFORTS

In recent decades, man has come to realize that there can be an end to the "take all" attitude. As such, he has made serious and important strides to "put back" some of what he has taken.

In regard to fishing, and especially where the redfish is concerned, man has made tremendous headway in the "putting back" phase. Texas has achieved great progress in this respect, and today is the undisputed world leader in efforts to stock redfish in saltwater.

The combined efforts of conservation-minded groups, businesses and state agencies paved the way for the world's first operational saltwater redfish hatchery in Texas. Specifically, the leaders in the project included the Gulf Coast Conservation Association, Central Power and Light Company and the Texas Parks and Wildlife Department. The historic facility is located at Flour Bluff, near Corpus Christi on the middle Texas Coast. It has been in successful operation since 1983.

At this writing, approximately 42.5 million redfish fingerlings and fry hatched in the John Wilson Redfish Hatchery have been stocked in Texas bays. Although the bulk of the stockings have been made in middle Texas Coast bays, every bay system on the coast has received a share of the fingerlings.

There are, of course, skeptics who raise the question as to how many of the fingerlings survive and grow to maturity so that they can breed in the wild. All we have are estimates, which range from a fraction of a percentage point to an optimistic 10 percent.

In a roundtable off-the-record discussion a couple of years ago, three marine biologists from three different agencies pegged the survival rate to maturity at "a realistic one percent."

One biologist summed it up like this: "The average mature female redfish will drop about 100,000 fertile eggs. Divide this into that 42.5 million figure and you get 425 spawnings. That's less than a drop in the bucket in comparison with the spawn in the wild.

"The stocking program is a big help," he added, "but you have to be realistic and realize that the return is not going to be what a lot of fishermen expect."

The bulk of the stockings were made in Texas mid-coast bays, primarily because these bays are reasonably small and are the easiest to monitor. You can't tag inch-long fingerlings. So what you do is run sample nets at designated periods and in designated areas, and then record the number of each size class taken. Fish from the same stocking effort will all be of similar size. Knowing the growth rate of redfish, the biologists can correlate the fish to the stocking from which they came.

REDS IN FRESHWATER

Texas is also the leader in stocking redfish in freshwater impoundments. This innovative part of the stocking program has brought the feisty redfish to fishermen throughout the state ... anglers who seldom get to fish coastal waters. So far, the fish have thrived and grown to considerable size in select freshwater areas. The only "minus" in this facet of redfish stocking is the fact that the species does not spawn or reproduce in freshwater. Thus, what this amounts to at the present time is "put-and-take" fishing.

Fishermen who have caught redfish in both freshwater and saltwater report there is no noticeable difference in the way the fish fight. There is, however, a difference in the way the fish feed.

Fishermen report reds in freshwater are more apt to grab a bait quick and be off. They say there is little lipping of the bait before ingestion. They also report redfish seem to be more willing to hit lures in freshwater impoundments. The most likely reason may be the fact that the water in freshwater impoundments is clearer than in saltwater bays or the surf. These same fishermen also report that when schools of reds work in shallow areas of freshwater impoundments they tend to make the water rather sandy as they root the bottom for aquatic life.

Redfish and black drum were released in Texas freshwater areas at least three decades ago. There are records noting releases in 1954, and according to talk, there were some private individuals who tried planting redfish in their lakes as early as 1950.

These small redfish were caught from the state's saltwater bays, trucked to the interior and subsequently released in freshwater impoundments, including a few rivers. All of the early releases involved small numbers of fish.

It was not until the Texas Parks and Wildlife Department's experimental hatchery at Palacios became operational that substantial numbers of redfish were released in select bodies of freshwater around the state. That pioneering facility, however, was geared toward research instead of production. The really big releases involving tens of thousands of fingerlings and fry became realities after the John Wilson Redfish Hatchery at Flour Bluff became operational.

The list of Texas freshwater impoundments that have received redfish, as well as black drum and red/black drum crosses, reads like the index to a travel map. A random list includes: Lake Braunig, the Brazos River, Lake Colorado City, Fairfield Lake, Hamlin Creek, Imperial Reservoir, Lake Kemp, Long Lake, Mountain Creek Lake, Lake Nasworthy, the Pecos River, Red Bluff Reservoir, Sheldon Lake, Striker Creek Reservoir, Tow Lake, Trading House Creek, White River Lake and White Rock Lake.

At the present writing Lake Braunig, situated just outside of San Antonio, offers the most consistent redfish action. It is recognized throughout the state as the freshwater impoundment to fish for large specimens.

Fish fry and fingerlings raised in Texas hatcheries have also been sent to a number of universities, including institutions in other states, for study. At this writing several other coastal states are considering starting up their own hatcheries for the purpose of stocking redfish in their territorial coastal waters. There is hope that in the decades to come redfish stocked in coastal waters may eventually extend the range of the species to that of former years.

TEXAS STOCKING PROGRAM

If at first you don't succeed, try, try again.

That dated piece of wisdom has long been the byword of redfish study and propagation for the Texas Parks and Wildlife Department. The state agency is the acknowledged forerunner in both freshwater and saltwater propagation of redfish.

Texas' work and study on the redfish certainly makes the species one of the most studied of saltwater fish. Colossal advancements were made in redfish propagation during the decade of 1980.

Those accomplishments, however, would never have become reality had not experimental work been done as far back as 1954. That was the year when redfish were first introduced, at least officially, into a Texas freshwater impoundment. Small redfish were caught from a Texas bay, and the catch was transported in

Daily bag, possession and length limits on redfish vary from state to state. Furthermore, those regulations are prone to change frequently as we learn more about the fish and how the fishery can best be managed. (Photo by Larry Bozka)

tanks to Kemp Lake in Central Texas. The redfish stocked that year totaled 58. This was followed a year later with a second stocking: 16 more redfish in Kemp and 500 in the Pecos River.

Kemp received additional stockings of 1,304 tiny reds in 1956 and four mature fish in 1957. Through 1966, annual stockings of redfish taken from coastal waters were introduced into the Pecos River, Red Bluff Reservoir and Imperial Reservoir. The largest stocking during that period took place in 1964, when 746 fish were released in Red Bluff Reservoir.

The first year of large stockings of fry, fingerlings and juvenile redfish was in 1975. The fish were raised in the state's saltwater hatchery at Palacios. Altogether, stockings that year totaled 12,319,936 fry, fingerlings and juveniles, plus a few mature reds. It was also the first year that stockings were made in bodies of saltwater, specifically Redfish Bay, Aransas Pass and Corpus

Christi Bay. Likewise, it was the first year in which fry and fingerlings were supplied to various universities for study. A total of seven freshwater impoundments received stockings that year. For the next five years, through 1980, the stocking program almost ground to a halt. The low was in 1979, when 19 fish were released in the Brazos River.

The program regained steam in 1981, when 1,149,674 fry and fingerlings were released in seven freshwater reservoirs. The total dropped to 660,110 in 1982, with a little over 100,000 going to Alabama and Florida for stocking and study.

The John Wilson Redfish Hatchery went on line in 1983, the first year that fry and fingerling stockings zoomed into the millions. Stockings in 1983 went to six freshwater impoundments, four saltwater bays, selected universities and the state of South Carolina.

A similar number in 1984 went into five saltwater bays and eight freshwater areas. That year another 1,000 were sent to South Carolina.

Beginning in 1985 and ever since, the largest stockings have been in saltwater areas. The 1985 total was 9,993,093, with 4,532,852 going into Espiritu Santo Bay and 1,237,399 going into the Lower Laguna Madre. The total for 1986 was 8,891,544, with the largest percentage going into 10 saltwater bays.

The 1987 stocking program accounted for the release of 35,182,270 fry and fingerlings into 14 saltwater bays and seven freshwater impoundments. The largest stockings were in South Bay at Port Aransas (14,872,678) and Aransas Bay (10,166,600).

Another 42,500,000 were stocked in 1988, although at the time of this writing, specific figures on the various bodies of water were not available.

Including the 1988 total, the grand total of redfish released in Texas waters, including those sent to other states for study, is 127,515,400.

That total includes the 58 fish that started it all back in Kemp Lake in 1954. **BB**

12.
THE BLACK DRUM

The black drum, Pogonias cromis, not only shares a range comparable to that of the redfish, but in fact is closely related. Along with the speckled trout and the golden croaker, the black drum and redfish are members of the croaker family. All of these fish have the ability to use their air bladders to make a croaking or drumming sound. (Photo by Larry Bozka)

o book on the redfish, or red drum, would be complete without several chapters on the black drum. The redfish and black drum are closely related. Along with the speckled trout and Atlantic croaker (Golden croaker), the fish is a member of the croaker family.

A common characteristic of this family is the ability of the fish to use their air bladders to make a croaking or drumming sound. This ability is most highly developed in the black drum, and it is so pronounced that a large black drum "drumming" when it passes very near or under a thin-hulled boat can be heard by the boat's occupants.

The black drum, *Pogonias cromis* to the marine biologists, has a range nearly as wide as that of the redfish. The fish ranges along the Gulf Coast states and up the Atlantic Coast as far north as New Jersey. Black drum are most abundant along the Texas and Louisiana coasts and the northern portions of both Florida coasts. The area of greatest abundance in Texas waters is from Galveston southward to Brownsville.

DESCRIPTION, CHARACTERISTICS

The black drum is built more for strength than for speed. Physically it is a chunky, high-backed fish with large, hard-spined fins. The general length of the fish is about three times that of its depth. The redfish is more elongated, and is approximately four-and-a-half times longer than its depth. The drum's scales are larger, and firmly attached.

Drum are bottom-feeders, and this is most evident from the many whiskers or "barbels" under the lower jaw. The fish uses these barbels to pick up scent and to feel its food. Young drum, which are often called "puppy drum," are the most vividly marked of the species, and these markings often cause newcomers to fishing to mistake it for a sheepshead.

A young drum has four to five dark vertical bars on its sides. The sheepshead has a deeper body, and has clearly defined black and white bars on its sides. The sheepshead's fins contain much harder spines than those found on drum.

The dark vertical bars on drum disappear with age, and mature drum may vary in color from a solid silver-gray to almost black. The belly of the fish is white, but the sides and back vary in color. Drum taken from open Gulf of Mexico or Atlantic Ocean waters usually lack distinct color, and tend to be light gray or silvery.

The black drum has no canine teeth like those of the speckled trout, but does have highly developed pharyngeal teeth. These "teeth" are actually located in the fish's throat, and enable it to crush crabs and mollusks before swallowing. (Photo by Larry Bozka)

Those that inhabit muddy bays have dark gray backs and sides that on occasion appear almost black.

Black drum are bottom-feeders that dine heavily on crabs and shell life, including oysters. As a matter of fact, schools of large drum have been known to ravage reefs containing high percentages of young oysters. Consequently, the black drum has few friends in the commercial oyster industry.

The fish lacks canine teeth, but its mouth is paved with heavy grinding teeth. It has highly developed pharyngeal teeth in the pharynx or throat, and the fish uses them to crush crabs and mollusks before swallowing.

SPAWNING, GROWTH

Within its range, the black drum is rather cosmopolitan in its spawning habits. Whereas the speckled trout spawns only in the bays and the redfish spawns only in the surf, the black drum readily spawns wherever it happens to be during its two spawning seasons. The first, and most important spawning season begins in late February and extends through March. The second is much shorter and takes place in June and July.

The black drum spawns in bays, offshore and in the channels, passes and cuts that connect these waters. It is also a free-spawning fish in that it randomly releases its eggs. The larval drum are found in the surf and along bay shorelines in March and April, and by mid-summer juvenile drum about an inch long are common in shallow bay areas.

Black drum grow rather slowly. The fish reaches approximately six inches in the first year, 12 inches in two years and 16 inches in three years. After that, the black drum increases about two inches a year. Unlike the redfish, of which most big specimens are females, large black drum can be either male or female. The largest black drum on record weighed 146 pounds. The Texas state record, caught in June of 1988, stands at 81 pounds. Most bull drum, however, range from 25 to 40 pounds.

Based on the average growth rate, drum in the current Texas slot lengths would range from two-and-a-half years (14 inches) to 10 years (30 inches).

Bag and slot length limits have been imposed on this fish because of increasing fishing pressure and a population that's been declining since the early 1980s. One of the reasons for the popularity of the fish is the fact that it is one of the few big fish that can be caught from the shore. Equally appealing is the fact that the black drum fisherman does not have to spend a lot of money on special gear.

Some of the most popular fishing tournaments in Gulf Coast waters are for black drum, and these tournaments are almost always held during the primary spawning run: late February through April.

One aspect of many of these tournaments, particularly in Texas and Louisiana, is awarding prizes for the most drum caught in a single day. This kind of competition is now restricted in Texas waters by the state's bag limit and maximum keeper length. The current Texas maximum keeper length of 30 inches rules out drum of approximately 10 years of age and older.

The black drum, again like the redfish, doesn't breed until it is approximately four to five years old. Using average growth rates, the black drum is capable of breeding when it is about 20 inches long.

FEEDING AND MIGRATION

The barbels on the black drum's chin indicate that the fish locates its food primarily by scent and feel, and that it is mainly a bottom-feeder.

Marine worms, small shrimp, small crabs and tiny fish make up the diet of young drum, specimens up to about three pounds. As the fish grow older, they feed more often on crabs, mollusks, marine worms, small fish and algae.

Drum, including the puppy size, often root out buried worms and mollusks by feeding in a head-down position. They commonly do this in water so shallow that their tails stick out of the water. Large drum working shallow areas in which marine worms may be plentiful are sometimes seen swimming along with their backs showing above the surface of the water.

The drum's habit of rooting the bottom head-down is very similar to the "tailing" of redfish. The two species engage in the same kind of feeding.

Schools of drum can change the configuration of the bottom. As they root along for food, they can change a smooth bottom into a moon-like surface pocked with numerous craters. Experienced fishermen can determine the passage of a school of drum by the large number of craters in an area. Old salts call the craters "drum noodles." Redfish, too, make craters, but not nearly as deep as or to the extent of the drum.

Drum migrations are directly influenced by the food supply and water conditions. When food is plentiful, there is very little migration. The most notable migrations are those associated with spawning and freshwater. The fish are very apt to move into areas where the water is quite fresh.

Movement between bay systems is very common. Drum frequently move into bays with lots of freshwater runoff. This migration may be triggered by the fact that fresh water sweeps a

Fishermen tend to confuse small drum for sheepshead, shown here. Note the sheepshead's vertical markings. Puppy drum also exhibit this characteristic, but lose the stripes prior to reaching maturity. (Photo by A.C. Becker, Jr.)

lot of land worms, insects and algae into such bays.

Drum will also move from one bay to another if there is a rise or fall in the mollusk population. They follow blue crabs, and whenever you find a big crab population in a bay you also find a lot of drum, including big 25-to 40-pounders.

A number of tagging studies have been made on black drum, and there are records of fish which have migrated up to 250 miles from the point of tagging. More realistically, however, the recovery of tags indicates these fish move less than several dozen miles throughout the course of a year.

The most common migration of black drum is from deep water to shallow and back. These are seasonal migrations. After the March-April spawning run along the Gulf Coast, the big drum begin to appear in deep offshore waters and continue to do so through the summer. Along the northeast Florida Coast, the fish

When used as drum bait, large crabs should be shelled and broken in half. Break off the pincher claws and drive the hook through one of the sockets until the point and barb are exposed. For maximum scent appeal, leave the fat and entrails intact. (Photo by A. C. Becker, Jr.)

show up in late February and remain through May. In the Cape May area on the south New Jersey Coast, the drum's first appearance is usually in May. The fish remains well through the summer in this area.

QUALITY AS FOOD

As a food fish, the black drum is very much underutilized. This is true throughout the range of the fish, in spite of the fact that it is a mainstay of the commercial fishery. The problem is that the fish as a table commodity is not well accepted by sport fishermen.

A good example of this can be found in many of the drum fishing tournaments. The contestants seldom keep the fish they catch. They give the meat away, usually to charitable groups.

Black drum as a species, meaning the puppy fish as well as the bulls, are victims of continuing "bad press." The fish doesn't get failing marks as far as being sporty to catch, but it is severely downgraded as far as table fare is concerned.

The small drum ... those under about five pounds ... certainly deserve better. Cleaned and properly prepared, the small drum is as good for table fare as the glamour fish like speckled trout, redfish, flounder and red snapper. In fact, there are coastal restaurants that feature puppy drum on their menus.

Large drum caught in the winter, and especially before spawning, are usually in better condition than those caught in the summer and after spawning.

Most fish species have worm infestations to some degree. For example, very small worms called "spaghetti worms" are reasonably common in speckled trout. But they are so tiny that they most often go unnoticed.

That's not the case with black drum. The bigger the drum, the bigger the worms. Instead of being very tiny and thread-like, the "spaghetti worms" found in large drum are truly spaghetti-size.

It's not an appetizing sight to dress a big black drum and find squiggly masses of worms in the flesh along the backbone. If they are well-cooked in the meat, the worms are not harmful to man, and in fact are reported to be rich in protein.

Meat free of the worms can be cut from the flanks or "saddle" of the fish. Saddle meat is meat from between the pectorals and the anal fin. The meat from small drum under about five pounds is firm, white and tasty. It can be broiled, or dipped into a batter and fried. Meat from large drum is coarse, dry and rather tasteless. Nevertheless, it can be quite good when used in a chowder. **BB**

13.
FISHING FOR SMALL DRUM

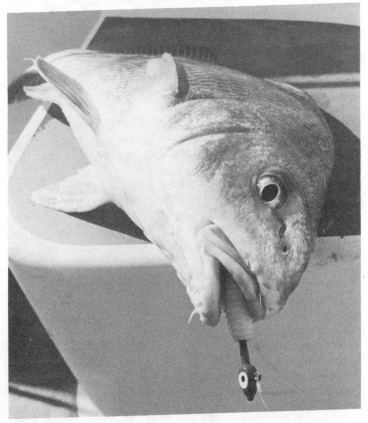

Small black drum are far more likely to hit artificial lures than their bull-class brethren. Few people fish artificials specifically for black drum, and most of the fish caught are taken by anglers throwing bottom-bumping grubs and shrimptails for redfish, speckled trout or flounder. (Photo by Larry Bozka)

Small drum to about five pounds make excellent table fare, and on light tackle can be very exciting to catch. They literally abound in areas where food matter is abundant. Areas rich in marine worms, crabs and mollusks are prime places to fish.

Especially productive are waters where the bottom is quite muddy. Equally rewarding fishing can be found around reefs, along the edges of saltgrass marshes and well up into bayous. The surf can be excellent when breakers are big enough to churn up the bottom, and with a good rolling surf you can often find small drum in water just a couple of feet deep.

During the warm weather months, small drum often school in bay waters so shallow that their backs show above the surface. Don't expect to see this at the height of the day, because they will beat a retreat to deeper water when the sun's rays beat down. Look for them on the flats and with their backs breaking the surface at night or under very poor light conditions.

If something spooks the fish when they are schooling in this manner the entire school will move almost as one. It is not uncommon for schools to cause swells on the water as the fish move across a flat. This usually happens when the water is very clear, a condition that makes drum quite spooky, based on personal experiences.

I feel that drum are almost as quick to spook as are redfish. The schools, however, are much less likely to leave if the water is off-color or murky. When drum are encountered in muddy water, the fish themselves are often the cause of the discoloration.

Drum are bottom-feeders, and they do a lot of grubbing, rooting and fanning the bottom for their food. People fishing for small drum should always be on the alert for patches of muddy water. You won't find these patches when the wind is brisk and the water is rough, but on a calm day, a drum fisherman can get into some exciting fishing simply by searching out muddy patches of water and then fishing the immediate area.

This kind of fishing is easiest for boaters. Instead of crossing the flats looking for slicks as when seeking speckled trout, the boaters look for patches of sandy to muddy water. If the water shows signs of having been muddied quite recently, you can expect to find small drum in the immediate area. The nice thing about this is that drum will linger in an area as long as there is food matter.

Black drum are not fast growers. The fish reach approximately six inches in the first year, 12 inches in two years and sixteen inches in three years. After that, the fish increase in size at a rate of roughly two inches a year. (Photo by Larry Bozka)

Years ago, a couple of old salts I used to fish with taught me how to find individual drum on the flats. They taught me to look for small muddy patches in which the mud or sand appeared to be boiling on the surface. This was always in water a couple or three feet deep.

They told me this was a drum, or several drum, in the act of rooting and fanning the bottom. The fishing technique then was to cast the bait right into the patch. There were times when I had drum strikes within seconds of when the bait hit the bottom.

There's a bonus in this kind of fishing, for sometimes the fish caught from the muddy patch turn out to be redfish. They, too, root the bottom, but not so vociferously as the drum.

DRUM NOODLES

Small drum advertise their presence to wade fishermen. They do it by the way they alter the configuration of the bottom.

As feeding schools root across a flat, they leave behind a mass of small depressions or craters. The fish don't seem content to merely pick food off the bottom. They also vigorously root the bottom to uncover what is buried in the sand and mud. The old salts call the craters "drum noodles."

The "noodles" range from about a foot to several feet in diameter, and in depth from a few inches to almost a foot. The small "noodles" are made by individual fish. The larger "noodles" are made by several fish working in unison. The deeper craters are usually found on muddy bottom areas, where drum often congregate in considerable numbers. This may be the reason some old salts call drum "muddy water" fish.

There's a technique waders can use when they find a flat pocked with "drum noodles." Wade and fish into the current. Drum, more than many species of fish, work and feed into the current. Hence, the school that cratered the bottom may be just upcurrent from the depressions you're stepping into. Move along slowly so as not to spook any fish that may be in the direction in which you're wading. If there is an abundance of food in the area, the school will remain close at hand, often working the same waters day after day.

Particularly good areas to fish for drum are in the vicinity of working oyster boats and channel dredging operations. The oystermen and dredgers churn up a lot of bottom, and with it comes a lot of what drum feed upon. The way to fish these areas is to note the direction in which the current carries the suspended sand and mud. Then get into position to fish the off-colored water as the current sweeps it by.

This same technique will sometimes pay off with redfish. The area to fish for reds, however, is along the edge of the muddy water ... not right in it, as you would for black drum.

BAITS TO USE

Although crabs, small oysters, clams and other mollusks are favorite foods of the black drum, the most rewarding baits when seeking small drum are shrimp, squid and cut bait. Peeled shrimp tails are particularly effective, the smellier the better. Obviously, the scent makes the bait easier to locate.

Small crabs just an inch or two long are good for puppy drum. However, getting an adequate supply can be time-consuming, since bait camps simply don't stock this kind of bait.

Based on personal experience, I have found that fish attractants can be a decided help when fishing for small drum. I have used those specially formulated for saltwater fishing, and have found them to be quite effective when the water is muddy. The scent carried along by the current gives the fish a sort of chum line to follow.

Small drum usually hit a bait harder than do the big bulls. This appears to be a trait of fish that travel in schools. When they are young, they have to be aggressive in taking their food or the rest of the fish in the school will leave them nothing. It is only when drum reach adulthood that they pick up a bait and lip it a few seconds before ingesting. Regardless of what kind of bait is used for small drum, the bait must be fished on or very near the bottom. If the bottom is mostly sand or mud, use either a fish-finder rig or a bottom rig with the sinker on the terminal end of the leader and two hook stagings above it. The fish-finder rig is best if there are currents.

Drum show an affinity for feeding around reefs, wrecks, docks, pier pilings and similar structure. Hence, a good rig to use in this situation is a single hook at the end of a leader fished under a float. Rig the float so the bait will be held just off the reef or structure.

The drum won't come all the way to the surface for the bait, but will rise a foot or two off the bottom if the bait is to their liking. A ripe, smelly shrimp tail, piece of equally ripe squid or chunk of cut bait is a good choice of baits when fishing under a float.

LURES FOR DRUM

The drum is not a fish that is normally pursued with lures, and it used to be believed that any drum caught on hardware was strictly an accident.

Today, however, some of the people who fish for drum have second thoughts. For one thing, the fish attractants have added scent to the appeal of lures. Another point is there are so many more people fishing lures these days that, even if drum take lures only by accident, an awful lot of accidents are occurring.

Based on personal fishing experiences, I believe a few types of lures have drum appeal. They include small spoons, small bottom-bumping plugs and bait-tails, especially the worm tails. I have found small drum are far more likely to take artificials than the big fellows.

I've had the most success with bait-tails rigged with soft plastic worm tails. Personally, I prefer to use four-to five-inch nightcrawler-type plastic worms rigged on a hook Texas-style as one would do when fishing for black bass. This is a very effective lure, especially when impregnated with scent attractants. This kind of lure is most effective when fished on a mud bottom or around reefs. The fishing technique is to inch it along slowly. When a pickup is felt, wait a few seconds before striking to set the hook.

The only problem with the plastic worm is that the fish's teeth render a worm useless after just a fish or two. The drum has crusher-type teeth, and the fish apparently grinds everything it eats.

THE RIGHT TACKLE

A bay popping rod with a light conventional wind, spinning or open-face reel is ideal for use on small drum. The fish does not make long runs, so there is really little problem in controlling the fish. Expect numerous runs, first in one direction and then in the other, but always toward the bottom.

A problem arises, though, at the mere mention of a popping rod and reel. Newcomers to puppy drum fishing immediately think in terms of speckled trout tackle. That's exactly what it is as far as the rod, reel and line are concerned. After that, the similarity stops. This is particularly true in the choice of hooks.

The treble hook that is so popular for speckled trout fishing is the wrong choice for drum, even those that are smaller than the minimum keeper length. These fish have teeth like cobblestones, and they have very strong jaw muscles. They crush and grind everything they eat.

If you use a treble hook, the fish will very likely mash it into a useless mass of twisted wire. Even if the hook beds somewhere in the fish's mouth and you land the fish, you will have to discard the hook and tie on a new one. That amounts to a lot of wasted time.

Instead, use a strong 2/0 to 4/0 single-tine hook for small drum. My personal preferences are forged O'Shaughnessy and Kirby hooks. These are strong hooks that are difficult to bend out of shape. During the course of a day's drum fishing, the fisherman needs to check the hook point for sharpness after every drum caught. Those cobblestone teeth will dull a hook in a hurry.

The drum has grinding teeth, not clipping teeth or canine teeth. Consequently, you can use monofilament for leader material. Use 20-to 30-pound test for small drum. Go with heavier mono, 50-to 60-pound test, to make leaders for bull drum. If the fish are taken from areas where there are a lot of sharp shells or structure that may chafe the leader, switch to wire leader. **BB**

14.
FISHING FOR
BULL DRUM

Deep holes on the edges of jetties attract not only redfish, but also big black drum.
Strong currents in deep-water channel areas necessitate the use of stout boat tackle
and heavy sinkers. (Photo by Larry Bozka)

Every fisherman entertains thoughts of catching a big fish. Desire and reality, however, can be poles apart, with the difference most often a matter of money. Set your sights on catching a big blue marlin or, on a closer-to-home basis, a glistening silver tarpon. Either way, it's going to be expensive.

The trip will be costly in specialized tackle, travel time, guide services, away-from-home accommodations, food and miscellaneous expenses. Too frequently, the final tally is so high you can't afford the luxury of going for the big one this year... or maybe not even next year.

Must the enthusiasm to catch a big fish wither on the vine? Not so, if you face fishing realistically and accept the fact that we can't always realize our dreams immediately. You can, however, do something to ease the pain.

Try focusing your attention on bull black drum, heavyweights that consistently run to 40 or 50 pounds, and on occasion, even more. These biggies are available not just once in a lifetime, but every year, and they can be caught without having to take out a second or third mortgage on the old homestead.

Heavyweight black drum can be, and are, caught on inexpensive bread-and-butter tackle. There is really no need for a boat, for the big ones can be caught from piers as well as from the surf. These big fish can be caught so inexpensively that the species truly deserves its reputation of being the ''working man's big game fish.''

It can even be caught tug-of-war style with tackle as simple as a handline. Let me briefly relate the story.

Back in the late 1930s it was a kind of teenage fad at Galveston to land a big fish with a handline. This was usually done from a pier or in the surf, and it wasn't specifically for drum but for any big fish that could be hooked.

Some of the guys caught sharks. I happened to catch three drum, which ranged in weight from 20 to about 30 pounds.

The tackle was a stout handline made of a hundred yards or so of 50-pound test line, a couple of 5/0 or 6/0 hooks and a heavy lead sinker. The technique was to tie the heavy sinker at the end of the line and then loop two hook stagings above it. The remainder of the line was wrapped around a length of broomstick.

The procedure was to wind off as much line as you could cast. The baited hooks and lead sinker were then whirled around your head and flung as far seaward as possible. From then on you simply waited for a fish to pick up the bait, holding the line in one hand and the stick with the remainder of the line in the other. And, of course, you wore cotton gloves on each.

When you hooked a fish you basically struggled with it, letting line slip out when the fish surged and then hauling it back in when the situation allowed.

It was a popular teenage fad at the time. We didn't have much money and there was little to do, so to pass the time we went handline fishing. If nothing else, the handline adventures should illustrate that you don't need expensive, state-of-the-art gear to catch some fish. It should also prove that "the working man's big game fish" sort of started out as "the poor boy's folly."

THE RIGHT TACKLE

But so much for youth's follies; let's get to bull drum fishing in earnest.

If you're fishing from a pier or in the surf, a long rod is an absolute must. You will need it to get distance when casting as well as leverage for turning and guiding stubborn fish. Arm it with a 4/0 to 5/0 reel filled with 30-to 40-pound-test line.

You really don't need a lot of line, but a full reel makes for easy casting. Actually, there is no need for more than a couple hundred yards of line because drum, even the big heavyweights, don't make long runs. They run back and forth, in and out, but rarely more than 20 or 30 yards at a time.

As a result, each time they change direction you can usually regain some line. The fish's most stubborn fight is always to get to the bottom, where it seems to be most at home.

The fight with a big drum is two-fold. First, you must keep a steady strain on the fish to sap its energy. Second, you must control its runs to keep the fish away from underwater structure that may foul the line or chafe it in two.

If you're fishing in deep water, as soon as you get the fish about halfway off the bottom you know you have it whipped. The sign of a surrendering drum is when the fish begins to come up and swim near the surface. If the fish turns on its side at the surface, it is ready for the gaff or landing net.

A big drum makes neither long nor fast runs. The body configuration, in particular the depth of the body, is not fashioned for fast swimming.

BAITS TO USE

Without question, the most critical point in fishing for bull drum is selecting the right bait. It is interesting to note that for the same size fish, the right bait for fishing the surf will differ from what is right to use in deep water.

When fishing the surf for big drum, use large shrimp, squid or cut mullet. Although drum readily feed on crabs, crabs do not make prime baits for surf fishing.

Regardless of what bait you use in the surf, it helps to douse or spray it with saltwater formulated fish attractant. Since the best drum action in the surf invariably takes place in sandy water, the reason for the use of an attractant should be obvious.

Now let's leave the surf and go for drum in deep water ... in channels, along jetties, and out from docks and piers which front on holes or cuts.

In order of effectiveness, use blue crabs, cut bait, large shrimp and squid. If the crab is small, with a carapace of three to four inches, place the creature on the hook live. Break off the pincher claws and insert the hook into one of the empty sockets. Turn the hook, and push it far enough through the body so that the point and barb will protrude out of the carapace.

Small blue crabs are not always available. If you are forced to use a large crab, be sure to break off the carapace as well as the pincher claws. Then break the body in two pieces to make two baits.

Again, drive the hook through one of the sockets and push it through until the point and barb is exposed. Leave the fat and entrails intact in the cavity. This aids in providing scent for the fish. Also, leave the fingers attached to the body, as they wiggle enticingly in a current and help to catch the fish's attention.

HOW BULLS STRIKE

Bull drum and bull redfish have more in common than just their membership in the croaker family. They take their food in similar fashion and obviously, because of their size, don't have to compete much with other fish for their meals. They are big enough to discourage intruders, and therefore go about their feeding in a leisurely manner.

Bull drum and bull redfish usually lip their food. They pick it up and appear to mouth it, testing to determine if it is edible. If it is to their liking, they will slowly swim off, carrying the bait in their

Blue crabs make up a major portion of the black drum's diet, and as such make excellent baits for deep-water drum fishing. Preferred baits for surf fishing are cut mullet, squid or large shrimp. (Photo by Larry Bozka)

mouths.

This is where drum and redfish part company. At this point the redfish will usually gulp down the food. The drum, on the other hand, will crush and grind it with all those cobblestone teeth. This is the time to rare back on the rod to bed the hook.

The fight of the bull drum is one of strong, dogged runs back and forth ... but always toward the bottom. If big drum would keep running in only one direction, many of them would win their freedom by simply stripping all the line from the reel and snapping it.

RELEASING DRUM

Many states in which black drum are found now have bag, possession and slot length limits. That means there may be many occasions when it is necessary to release your catch. Do it the right way, and the fish will survive. Do it haphazardly, and there will be a very high mortality rate.

The black drum is a hearty fish, but it is not so robust that it can be callously handled. Special care is necessary, particularly if the fish is a big one taken from deep water.

Simply taking the fish off the hook and throwing it overboard will not do the job. The fish will not be able to return to the bottom unless its swim bladder, known by some as the "air bladder," is punctured.

The swim bladder is an internal organ that the fish inflates or deflates to compensate for changes in water pressure which occur as it swims deeper or shallower. It allows a fish to suspend itself motionless at any depth. Without the swim bladder, the fish would have to swim non-stop or otherwise sink to the bottom.

Sharks have no swim bladders, and as a result their lifestyle is literally one of "swim or sink." The flounder is another popular fish which shares this trait.

The swim bladder is an internal organ located on the lower body of the fish, immediately behind the pectoral fins. Puncture the side of the fish with a thin, sharp instrument, preferably an ice pick. A puncture of about an inch deep is sufficient on a large drum.

Yes, the fish will bleed a little, but the wound will quickly heal and the fish will survive. The puncture in a puppy drum need only be about a half-inch deep. If the fish is caught from shallow water and there are no deep holes in the immediate area, the fish can be released without the puncture.

The longer the fish is kept out of the water, the less its chance of survival. The time should be just a few minutes, certainly not more than five minutes at the most. If photos are to be taken, have the camera ready before the fish is removed from the water.

If the fish is to be weighed, hold it in a manner that supports its entire body. A sure way to kill a fish is to hang it up by its lips or head. A heavy fish hung in such a manner will suffer severe

Often referred to as "the working man's big game fish," black drum are common catches on beachfront fishing piers. Rather than making long runs, the fish tend to bore toward the bottom when hooked. (Photo by A.C. Becker, Jr.)

internal injuries, as its internal organs will shift and sag.

You can pretty well look at a fish in the water and determine whether or not it is a keeper. Some people consider it sporting to play a fish for a long time, but again, this is an almost certain way to kill your catch.

As the fish uses up energy in its efforts to escape, lactic acid forms in its muscle tissue. Such a fish may appear healthy when it is released, but because of lactic acid poisoning will usually die within a few hours.

Finally, don't release a fish into the water by throwing it overboard. Release it in an upright position, and if necessary, move it back and forth to create a flow of water through its gills. This will stimulate the fish's respiration.

When fish are handled and released carefully, the survival rate is right at 90 percent.

It's well worth the extra effort. **BB**

AFTERWORD

It is with sincere gratitude that we recognize the many friends who have done so much to make our first year a success.

Amidst a half-dozen priority deadlines and working mostly in the middle of the night, art director John Hillenbrand both conceptualized and implemented the design and layout of this book. His ability to work under intense pressure with confidence and poise is nothing short of amazing.

Friendswood, Texas artist Mark Mantell once again graciously applied his talents to the cover. Mantell's unique style is fast winning fans throughout the Gulf Coast, and we're honored to feature his work on this title.

Modern-day publishing is the product of computers. Getting them to function in a continuous and reliable fashion is often a challenging and complicated task. Doug Corry and David Wilson of Intervisions, Inc. saw to it that ours didn't miss a step.

Time is a precious commodity, and the following people generously donated theirs while manning our boat show booths and helping out at seminars. Special thanks to June Becker, Douglas Bolduc, Terri and Ron Frasier, Freda Katz, Pauline Katz and Richard Richardson. Richardson's prowess as a catcher of trophy king mackerel is surpassed only by his talents behind a video camera.

Special thanks, too, to video producer Bob Ball and Eileen Odell, who along with Richardson and my wife, Mary, handled the set-up and shooting of the May 6 speckled trout seminar in the face of a grueling schedule.

Our meeting room, reserved the prior night for a policeman's ball, wasn't ready for move-in until 4:00 a.m. The aforementioned crew did a day's work in less than four hours, assembling and testing a veritable maze of cables, cameras, monitors and recorders. They pulled it off with minutes to spare, and spent the following eight hours rolling tape.

Many thanks, also, to Houston Academy store manager Alan Richardson and Port O'Connor fishing guide James Helms, who at day's end volunteered to stay late and help us tear down and load the equipment.

Finally, our heartfelt appreciation to the thousands of Gulf Coast fishermen who have provided us the means to turn dreams into realities.

It's our hope that the next time your bait hits the water, what you learn from this book will do the same for you.

Larry Bozka   Houston, Texas

INDEX

124

OTHER BOOKS BY A.C. BECKER, JR.

Waterfowl in the marshes
(A.S. Barnes, 1969)

Gulf Coast Fishing
(A.S. Barnes, 1970)

Lure Fishing
(A.S. Barnes, 1970)

Big Red/Channel Bass Fishing
(A.S. Barnes, 1972)

Game and Bird Calling
(A.S. Barnes, 1972)

Decoying Waterfowl
(A.S. Barnes, 1973)

Fishing the Texas Coast
*(Cordovan Corp., 1975,
Second printing June, 1981)*

Texas Saltwater Big Three
*(Cordovan Corp., 1976,
Revised edition, 1976)*

The Complete Book of Fishing
(A.S. Barnes, 1977)

A.C. Becker's Speckled Trout
*(BOZKABOOKS, 1988
Second printing, March 1989)*